Praise for **Lead Ir**

"**Lead Inside the Box** is a must-read for leaders at any level. The concept of optimally investing your 'leadership capital' to get the best results from your team is a differentiator between good and great leaders. The practical and simple methods in this book will help you make much wiser investments and get better results."

—**Jim Hinrichs, Chief Financial Officer, CareFusion**

"Finally, a leadership book that cuts through all of the noise, theories, and models out there to deliver a practical approach to lead, motivate, and engage today's diverse, multi-generational workforce for maximum results. In an ever-changing global marketplace where leaders have to do more with less and do it faster than ever before, this book gives you the tools to effectively manage your people and to elevate them to new levels of performance and success. This book needs to be on every leader's desk!"

—**Andrea Procaccino, Chief Learning Officer, NewYork-Presbyterian Hospital**

"Leaders are consistently being asked to do more with less. **Lead Inside the Box** provides leaders with a simple yet effective construct for more efficiently spending their time and energy with their people to get significantly better results. Victor Prince and Mike Figliuolo have provided a realistic approach for being a better leader."

—**Sean Huffman, president, OhioHealth Neighborhood Care**

"One of the most difficult tasks in leading a team is making sure you're getting peak performance from each individual. This book provides simple tools not only to assess each team member, but also to guide them to be better contributors to bottom-line results. The authors' rich management experiences and real-life examples convey the effectiveness of their easy-to-follow methods for a better-functioning team."

—Connie Tipton, president and CEO, International Dairy Foods Association

"I've seen many overly complicated leadership models in my career. **Lead Inside the Box** breaks that mold and gives leaders something simple yet practical that they can use every day to improve their team's performance."

—Mark Naidicz, vice president, Human Resources & Employee Relations, AbbVie

"**Lead Inside the Box** offers fresh and practical advice for leaders looking to get better results out of their teams. I highly recommend it."

—Amit Chatterjee, EVP of CA Technologies, *Fortune* magazine's "40 under 40" 2010 Awardee

"A business leader's most crucial charge is to effectively manage people and time. Victor Prince and Mike Figliuolo provide a potent yet practicable tool targeted directly at the intersection of this dual mission."

—Tom Macina, CEO of Mesirow Advanced Strategies, Inc.

"If you want to see your team in a new way, and find new approaches to leading and motivating them, Victor Prince and Mike Figliuolo have developed a framework that will enable you to do exactly that. The guidance is practical and can be applied to the leadership challenges you face every day. My experience leading teams that work across the globe and across the hall tells me that this book would have helped me from the beginning to be a better leader. With all the pressures leaders face, we must find new ways to lead our teams more effectively. **Lead Inside the Box** gives leaders a model of not just being effective but also being efficient—time we all surely need. This is a great fundamental read for every leader and team member no matter what level you are at."

—Rob Miller, divisional vice president, R&D and Scientific & Medical Affairs, Abbott Nutrition

"Victor Prince's and Mike Figliuolo's real-world experiences fill the pages of **Lead Inside the Box** and their perspectives will immediately help you lead your team more effectively."

—Paul Smith, author of *Lead With a Story* and *Parenting With a Story*

"This book comes at a critical juncture when 'doing more with less' doesn't work for organizations already thinned down during the last recession. It teaches you how to lead yourself, and your team, to thrive in today's economic climate."

—Leah Treat, director of Portland OR Bureau of Transportation

"Real-life leaders will find that **Lead Inside the Box** tackles their biggest real-life problem: getting the most out of their teams without sacrificing every last bit of creativity, energy, and time in the process. Leadership is an investment; Prince and Figliuolo help us invest wisely."

—Raj Date, managing partner, Fenway Summer LLC; former Deputy Director, U.S. Consumer Financial Protection Bureau

"All leaders want their team to shine, but people development is often one of the most frustrating and difficult roles of a leader. In their excellent new book, Mike Figliuolo and Victor Prince show how to focus your most precious resource—your own time and energy—to ensure the people you lead maximize their potential as individuals and as a team."

—Jesse Lyn Stoner, coauthor of *Full Steam Ahead!*

"If you're looking for a straightforward and actionable guide to untangling the complexities of leading a team, **Lead Inside the Box** is it. Figliuolo and Prince draw on their experience as executives and leadership coaches to give you a guide that you'll refer back to again and again."

—Scott Eblin, author of *The Next Level* **and** *Overworked and Overwhelmed: The Mindfulness Alternative*

"I have been a fan of Mike Figliuolo's work for some time because I have found his research solid and insights sparkling. His new title, **Lead Inside the Box**, coauthored with Victor Prince, is an exceptional addition to Figliuolo's body of work. **Lead Inside the Box** provides cogent advice about exactly how to lead from the middle (as well as the top) in ways that enable managers to make good things happen and help the organization prosper. The book contains workable models coupled with incisive questions that will help leaders figure things out for themselves and their teams. With research to back up their findings, Figliuolo and Prince's **Lead Inside the Box** is a resource everyone in leadership—or who aspires to leadership—will want on their bookshelves."

—John Baldoni, leadership expert and author of
MOXIE: The Secret to Bold and Gutsy Leadership

LEAD
INSIDE
THE BOX

LEAD
INSIDE
THE BOX

How
SMART LEADERS
Guide Their
Teams to
EXCEPTIONAL
RESULTS

Victor Prince and Mike Figliuolo

CAREER
PRESS

Wayne, N.J.

LEAD INSIDE THE BOX
EDITED AND TYPESET BY KARA KUMPEL
Cover design by Ty Nowicki
Printed in the U.S.A.

To order this title, please call toll-free 1-800-CAREER-1 (NJ and Canada: 201-848-0310) to order using VISA or MasterCard, or for further information on books from Career Press.

The Career Press, Inc.
www.careerpress.com

Library of Congress Cataloging-in-Publication Data
Prince, Victor.
    Lead inside the box : how smart leaders guide their teams to exceptional results / Victor Prince, Mike Figliuolo.
        pages cm   8/15
    Includes index. 60527933
        ISBN 978-1-63265-004-7 (paperback) -- ISBN 978-1-63265-995-8 (ebook)
1. Leadership. 2. Teams in the workplace. I. Figliuolo, Mike, 1970- II. Title.

HD57.7.P756 2015
658.4'092--dc23

2015010091

For Mom and Dad—for everything.
—Victor Prince

For Mom and Dad—words can't express.
—Mike Figliuolo

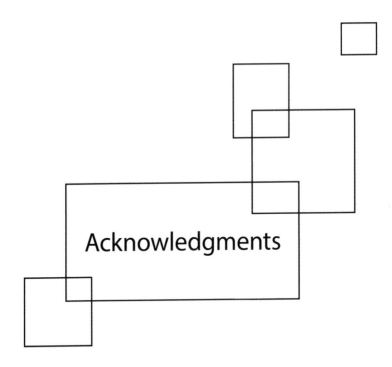

Acknowledgments

Victor Prince:

Pat and Gale—for leading me by example my whole life.

Tina—for inspiration.

Mike—for a wonderful partnership.

Giles Anderson—for being my favorite literary agent.

Adam Schwartz and the rest of the Career Press team—for making this happen.

Alexander and Charles—for blazing the trail for authors in the family.

Amy G., Bob B., Bruce E., Catherine W., Dan D., Dan T., Dean D., Jerry Y., Judith R., Katherine B., Liddy M., Neil A., Paul W., Ray B., Rich C., and Rich W.—for teaching me leadership firsthand by being a great boss, teacher, or coach to me at some point in my life.

To all my family and friends who asked me at some point about how "The Book" was coming along—writing a first book is a lonely, uncharted trek with no guaranteed finish line. Even the smallest gestures of interest and support meant more than you realized.

Mike Figliuolo:

Danielle, Michael, and Alexandra—Don't know what I'd do without your love, support, humor, and perspective. You're my treasures.

Mom and Dad—I appreciate all you've done and who you are more every day.

Gina—a million thanks to for the smiles and love. I still laugh every time I make mashed potatoes or waffles.

Nana, Pop, Grandma, and Grandpa—not only did you love me unconditionally, you taught me a person can be kind and humble while still being special.

The rest of my family—every single one of you is crazy in the most wonderful way. I couldn't ask for more perfect company. I love all of you.

Victor—thank you for including me in your idea and for being a great writing partner.

J. and T.—your continued guidance is a blessing.

Giles Anderson—your persistence, encouragement, and guidance are invaluable.

Adam Schwartz and the Career Press team—thank you for giving us the opportunity to share our passion for leadership with the world.

My teachers and coaches—for filling my head and my heart with wonderful knowledge.

Dr. Chapekis and the OhioHealth Team—for literally saving my life so I could be around to write this book (among other things).

My leaders—for teaching me what it means to lead and for setting a great example.

My team members—wow. Thanks for supporting me and always making me look good.

My clients—you make living the dream of my present career possible.

My friends and colleagues—I'm blessed that those two titles are synonymous.

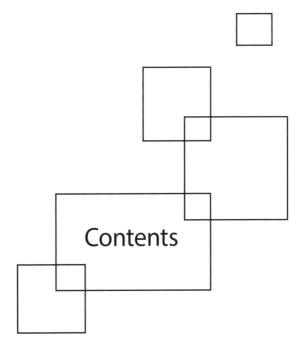

Contents

Part III: Leading Exemplars

Part IV: Leading High-Cost Producers

Part V: Leading Passengers

Part VI: Leading Detractors

Part VII: Applying the Leadership Matrix

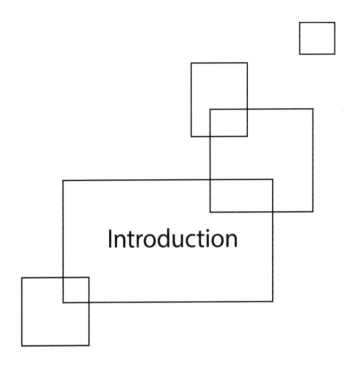

Introduction

During our early formal business education, we learned a model for how to allocate our company's cash if we ever found ourselves leading a global diversified conglomerate with a portfolio of companies. Something about cows, dogs, and stars...no mention of people, though, interestingly enough. For better or worse, neither of us ended up as the CEO of Global Conglomerate, Inc. We both have, however, led people on teams of varying sizes—from small strategy teams to large operationally focused business units. In those roles, we've found that cash isn't always the scarcest resource leaders have to invest—the time and energy it takes to lead people is. We refer to this limited resource as "leadership capital." There are only so many hours in a day, after all, and leaders can only push themselves so hard. At some point, leaders run out of leadership capital. When that happens, their performance and the performance of their teams will suffer. Figuring out how to manage one's own leadership capital is an important challenge.

The pressure on leaders increases every day. Calls to "do more with less" echo through the halls. Ever-escalating expectations create a great deal of stress for leaders. At the same time, *their* bosses are stressed, leaving less time for leaders to get the support they need. The options for delivering on these heightened expectations are limited. Sure, leaders can step on the proverbial gas pedal and work harder and longer to create more leadership capital, but time, after all, is a non-renewable resource. Play those games too long and the stress adds up. Leaders end up paying the price by taking away from other important things in their lives—their families, their hobbies, and their health. The cumulative effects of these stressors can be devastating.

When leaders overwork themselves, their teams tend to do the same. People stay at the office until the boss leaves. They respond to the boss's Sunday morning emails. Their stress levels are correlated with that of their boss. Eventually, team members get burned out in such an environment. The quality of their work declines. Their energy and morale plummet. They look for new jobs that will be less stressful. When they quit, they leave their leader shorthanded with an open role to fill. That vacancy increases the leader's stress and puts an additional burden on the other team members to pick up the slack. The negative performance spiral picks up speed with no sign of slowing down.

You may have gotten stressed out just reading about this hypothetical situation. That's because it's all too real. This brute-force approach to increasing leadership capital isn't sustainable.

If you want to avoid the problems that come from overworking yourself and your team, the only viable option is to be more efficient with how you spend your time and energy. How can you be smarter about how you're investing your energy to get the best results at work while still having a life outside of it? We'll give you a means to understand how you're investing your leadership capital. That understanding will give you a roadmap for being more thoughtful about those investments going forward.

Why are we writing this? Each of us has more than 20 years of experience leading and being led. We've both learned a great deal—many times, the hard way—by being on both sides of the leader–led relationship. We have experienced the thrills of leading high-performing teams and the pain of failing to lead well in challenging situations. We have also experienced the joy of being led well and the pain of being led poorly. We've been through many situations that have taught us the risks of pushing ourselves beyond our limits. Mike even had a heart attack partially as a result of not keeping himself in balance. He was pushing himself too hard and taking on too much stress. It's hard to lead people from a hospital room. We believe the lessons we've learned and the approaches we've come to appreciate can help other leaders be more successful leading their teams. We feel a profound obligation to share these ideas in the hope that we can improve other leaders' work performance and the quality of their lives. If only we were given a book like this when we took on our first leadership roles! Many challenges we faced, or even created due to our failures, could have been resolved more effectively.

Part I:
Introducing the Leadership Matrix

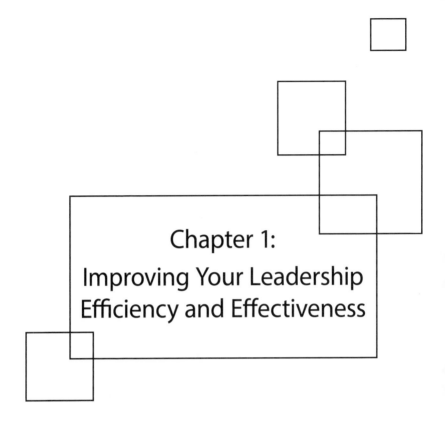

Chapter 1:
Improving Your Leadership Efficiency and Effectiveness

You don't fully control where and how you spend your leadership capital. Your investment of it is dictated by the behaviors of those around you. Team members can be demanding. They make mistakes that require your intervention. They cause conflicts that you have to smooth over. Alternately, they may ask little of you. You see them so infrequently that you occasionally forget they're there. Some of them hope you ignore them because your attention only means more work for them. Your boss or other leaders in the organization may require you to spend your time and energy a certain way. They might ask you to coach or mentor someone. They could decide to reorganize your department or reprioritize your projects. Those changes force you to spend time with different team members working on new tasks. Sure, you've got *some* control over how you invest your leadership capital, but don't fool yourself—much of the world around you is beyond your control.

What you *do* control, however, is your reaction to those behaviors and events. Just because one of your team members is clamoring for your time to solve his problems, it doesn't mean you have to give it to him. Instead, you can ask him to spend time on his own developing a solution and coming up with the best plan he can, and only once he's done so will you give him the time to sit down with you to review his solution. If you solve his problems every time he asks, you're enabling his bad behavior. For team members like this, it becomes far simpler for them to ask you to figure out the solution instead of investing their own time and energy to do so. You're rewarding their laziness. The more you reward it, the more frequently you'll be a victim of their inaction. All your leadership capital will be consumed by doing their job for them. Once you appreciate how much you're investing in the relationship, you can take different actions. You can reallocate that leadership capital to endeavors that will generate better results. That's this method's true power: it shows you how you're investing your time and energy and links those investments to the results you're getting.

Understanding Where You're Investing Leadership Capital

Through a set of simple questions, you can diagnose how you're investing your leadership capital. These questions will give you a good sense for where you spend your time and energy with your team members. You'll know whom you're investing in and whom you're ignoring. You can only reallocate your leadership capital and invest it more efficiently if you know where you're spending it in the first place.

Then, through another set of questions, you can assess the return you're getting from those investments. You pay your team members a salary to deliver results, but that's not the only investment you're making in them; you're also spending your leadership capital to get results. It's important to understand the return you get from *all* the investments you're making in your team. Some team members deliver more results than others, and they all have different styles for delivering those results. By analyzing the quality and quantity of results and the way they deliver them, you'll better understand the types of leadership interventions best suited to improving their performance. Ultimately, their results are a measure of your success. The more you can get out of them, the more valuable your team becomes. Their better results improve the organization's performance. Leaders who can make these improvements by *shifting* resources instead of *adding* them are more effective and more valuable, and have a brighter future than those who throw more of their limited time and energy at improving performance.

Once you know how you're investing your leadership capital and have a sense of the results being delivered by each team member, you have to understand how your efforts are—or aren't—contributing to those results. It's that causal relationship between your investment and their results that's the crux of this method. To evaluate that relationship, we'll provide a framework called the Leadership Matrix where you can plot your team members in one of four boxes that describe the behavioral patterns they demonstrate. A person's placement on the Leadership Matrix is a function of how much leadership capital that person requires you to invest compared to the results she delivers. Similar to financial investing, your goal is to get the highest return possible on the investments you make in your team members. As you perform these suggested analyses, you may shift where you're spending your time and energy to improve your team's performance. These shifts will occur because some team members need more of your attention while others require less. The reallocation of leadership capital is a major insight that comes out of this assessment process.

For each behavior type, we'll offer specific leadership techniques to use to target your efforts for that team member. For example, some people need you to be directive and monitor their work. Others will be better off if you leave them alone and check in less frequently. The idea is to apply the appropriate leadership techniques that best suit each individual's needs. We'll show you what these behaviors and techniques look like in the real world through extensive use of examples drawn from our personal experiences as well as our knowledge of leadership challenges faced by our colleagues and clients. These stories will demonstrate what this method looks like in practice and make it easier for you to use these techniques when you face similar situations. They also illustrate both good and bad ways to lead team members in each box and how you can use this method to be a more effective leader.

Using this approach will not only help you get the most out of your team, but it will also help your individual team members reach their true potential and be more satisfied with their jobs. By identifying their unique needs, you can tailor your leadership style to help them reach their personal and professional goals. When your team members feel valued as individuals and believe they're making progress on their career path, you're much more likely to get better results from them and have a healthier team environment. People tend to stay in jobs in such an environment and not look for other roles outside of your team. That dynamic's benefits are clear—less attrition, less work needing to be taken on by others during a vacancy, and less time spent recruiting and training new people. That positive cycle leaves more time for delivering better results or for achieving a better work-life balance.

The Benefits of Leading Inside the Box

Most leaders feel a duty to help their team members improve their performance, but soon realize that doing so is hard work. There's not always a clear path to achieve that improvement. Helping someone change his performance requires thoughtful evaluation of the situation and a willingness on the leader's part to use techniques that are tailored for that specific case. These techniques may be uncomfortable for the leader to apply. Many times, rather than trying something new, leaders resort to techniques they're already comfortable with. But one size does not fit all when it comes to the most effective leadership style for different types of team members.

Unfortunately, we establish our own routines, habits, and preferences for how we lead people, and it's difficult to break out of that mold for different situations. What those habits lead to is using the same leadership approach with all team members regardless of that technique's appropriateness for a particular situation. Although that common approach may work occasionally, more often than not it frustrates the team member. The leader is left wondering why performance isn't changing despite her use of an approach that has "always worked in the past." To inspire lasting performance improvement, a leader needs to lead her team members based upon the team member's needs—not the leader's comfort level.

Another trap leaders fall into is being reactive—leading team members in a way they ask for but may not need. Leaders often ask team members to do something challenging—change their behavior. Change is always

stressful and often difficult. Team members try to minimize the amount of change they have to suffer through.
One way team members do so is guiding their boss to
lead them in a certain way using techniques that feel comfortable for them. Those techniques might not be the
most appropriate for the situation. If, for example, a team
member needs to be held accountable for daily results but
the leader gives in to a request to "give me space and let
me manage my own work," disaster could result. While
team member preferences are important, the leader must
choose the most effective means of improving performance even if the team member won't like it.

The "leading inside the box" method we're advocating
shows leaders how to take a much more thoughtful, proactive approach to leading their team members to get the
best out of them while at the same time easing their burden of leadership. Said differently, this method is about
getting the greatest results out of your team members by
being wise about how you invest your time and energy.
This approach centers on a framework, but it's not about
labeling people and putting them in boxes. It's about cat-
egorizing the *behavioral characteristics* people demonstrate
and adapting your leadership style to change those behaviors. The better a leader tailors his leadership style
to each individual, the more likely it is that true behavior
change will occur.

Placement in a box on the Leadership Matrix is driven
by the behaviors of both the team member and the leader.
Those behaviors can change over time. People don't always stay in one box after they're placed there initially.

They can move by changing behaviors—especially if they're led effectively. They can also move within the Leadership Matrix by changing jobs. Both of us have been in every one of these boxes at different points in our careers. There are many examples of people who didn't find professional success until they moved out of jobs for which they were not well-suited. The world famous chef Julia Child, for example, was fired from her first job in advertising before she discovered her love of cooking in her late 30s. People sometimes find themselves in places they might not want to be. A leader's job is to help people move to a position of improved performance and increased satisfaction. To do that, leaders need to use different leadership approaches and target their efforts according to the individual's development needs. Setting a baseline for how people are performing and how the leader is interacting with them defines the starting point for performance-improvement efforts. Once that starting point is known, it's much clearer what needs to be done to sustain or improve performance. That knowledge enables leaders to reduce the amount of leadership capital they must invest to get the desired results.

There is no "end goal" box in the framework. Growth doesn't stop once someone reaches a "high performer" box. Leaders should be moving high performers on to new challenges as much as they try to help low performers move to a position of satisfactory performance. The "lead inside the box" approach is all about continuous performance improvement. Leaders must develop their people, get better results, and be more efficient in the process of making these improvements. Leaders who develop their people will find themselves with expanded opportunities to lead more people and take on more challenging assignments. Those new situations help leaders advance their careers and have a larger positive impact on the organization. In turn, these dynamics result in happier leaders who feel professionally and personally satisfied with their roles.

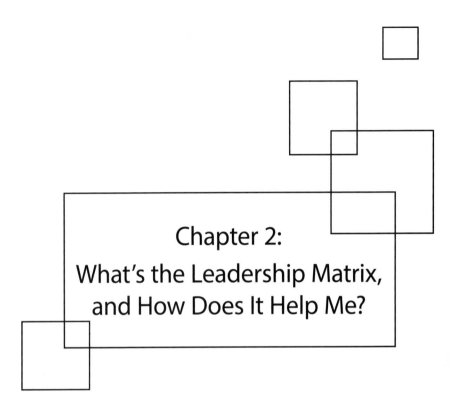

Chapter 2:
What's the Leadership Matrix, and How Does It Help Me?

Congratulations! If you're reading this you've either reached the ranks of leadership or you're well on your way there. Throughout the course of your career so far, you've likely navigated through a succession of jobs in team environments. But once you're responsible for leading others, the game changes. When you lead a team, you're not controlling all the effort that goes into the work and the quality of the output. Leaders have to manage that indirectly through their team members.

For some newly minted leaders, making the shift from delivering the work to working through others to deliver results feels like they've gone from pulling all the strings to pushing a rope. If they can't get their team members to do the job exactly the way they would do it, they may be tempted to micromanage or, even worse, do the work themselves. But now that they have more responsibilities, they can't do it all. If they take that approach, they'll burn themselves out and fail to deliver the results they desire and that the organization expects. Your scarcest resource is the time and energy available for you to invest in leading your team—your leadership capital. To get the most out of your team without burning yourself out, invest your leadership capital wisely. To do so, figure out where to invest it in your team members to achieve the greatest results for your efforts.

Different types of team members require different amounts and types of leadership capital from you. Being a smart leader means you proactively figure out how to invest your leadership capital instead of dedicating it to the most pressing performance issue or crisis. When we face a crisis, we tend to react first and think later—this might solve the immediate problem, but it could also cause dysfunctional behaviors to arise in your team members. If you behave this way often enough, you might become an enabler of bad behavior: rather than solving problems themselves, your team members will come to you to resolve their issues. Their demands will then take up all your time and energy. Why would they solve the difficult issues themselves when they can pass them off to you instead? They'll do this because this approach makes their lives easier. Avoid the mistake of always leading your team members exactly how they ask to be led. There will be occasions when you'll need to lead them much differently than they might desire. Don't let them dictate how you spend your leadership capital. It's *your* job to determine where you focus your energies.

Another common leadership capital allocation error to avoid is spreading your time and energy evenly across all your team members. Some people need a great deal of your attention. Others perform better if you leave them alone the majority of the time. Knowing the difference and acting accordingly requires effort on your part, but it's worth figuring out. Be thoughtful about how you allocate your efforts, rather than being lazy and doing what others ask you to do or parceling out your energy equally to everyone because that's a "fair" way to do it.

What Reallocating Leadership Capital Looks Like in Action

Let's look at an example of enabling behaviors and how they can drain a leader. A few years ago, Mike took on an assignment to be an executive coach for Alan, a seasoned executive who was considered a high performer. Alan leads a team of highly intelligent scientists. While most of their time is spent on scientific work, a portion of their roles is administrative. Before Alan took over the team, many of these scientists hadn't been trained on these responsibilities because their previous leader tended to do all this administrative work himself. Alan fell into that same habit when he took over the team.

During a hectic period, Alan and I spoke about how stressed out he was. "I don't have enough hours in the day to get all this stuff done," he said. When I asked what he was working on, he shared that he was performing these administrative tasks. As I pressed him for an answer as to why he was doing this work instead of making his team members do it, he said, "They've never been trained on it and they screw it up pretty often. I then have to fix those errors. When they *do* try to do it, they're constantly in my office asking me for answers to the problems they need to solve. It's more efficient for me to do the work myself rather than spend time I don't have trying to train them on how to do it properly."

I told him he was causing all the problems. "Do you know what the problem is, Alan?" I asked. "You're an enabler. Your behaviors are the root of the problem." Needless to say he was surprised by my unsympathetic response to his plight. "What's easier for them, Alan—to struggle with the work and suffer through the rework you'll demand of them or to claim they don't have the skills and dump the work on your desk instead?" Alan's eyes widened with the painful realization of the dynamic he had created. I continued, "Here's another thing to consider—how many hours have you spent doing this work in the last six months? How much time would it take you to train them on these tasks so you didn't have to spend the time doing them yourself?" He knew he didn't need to answer my questions. I offered a final perspective. "I know they're going to whine when you tell them to do the work. They're going to give you half-assed results in the hopes you'll capitulate and do it yourself instead of holding them accountable for doing it again. You have to break this cycle. Short-term, it will suck. They won't like you. You'll be less efficient because you'll be correcting more errors and spending more time training them than you would spend if you did the work yourself. Long-term, we both know you need to make this shift."

Alan stepped up to the challenge. When they brought him imperfect work, instead of picking up the black pen to do the work correctly, he reached for the red pen and marked the document up with the corrections he wanted them to make. He set a clear expectation that he would no longer be doing the work—they were only to come to him once they had a finished product. He made extensive correction marks on many deliverables. He listened to a great deal of groaning. He spent many hours teaching them *how* to do the work instead of doing the work for them. After his team members realized he wasn't going to revert to old habits, they gave in and improved the quality of their work. For them, Alan made it more efficient to do the work right the first time rather than suffer through his red pen and additional hours of instruction on how to do things right. After making this shift, Alan found he had more time available for working on higher-priority projects. He delivered better work, spent more time thinking about strategic issues, and stepped into larger responsibilities, which, in turn, advanced his career. His reallocation of his leadership capital enabled this transformation of the team dynamic from dysfunctional to effective.

Determining Where to Invest Leadership Capital

How do you determine how to invest your leadership capital? The same way you would look at any other investment—how much output do you get, and how much input does it take to get it? You can review your team members this way too. Assess how much output you get (the quality and quantity of their results) from the input they require from you (your leadership capital). Plotting those two "metrics" relative to one another creates a 2x2 matrix of four boxes that describe different types of team member behaviors (see the next page).

Your team is a portfolio of team members distributed across these different behavior types. If you're lucky, the majority of your team can be plotted in the upper right portion of the Leadership Matrix. That's where you get a large amount of high-quality results with little effort required from you. It's the most efficient place on the matrix. But more often than not, you'll find your team members are scattered across multiple boxes. Regardless of where they plot initially, remember, their position isn't fixed. As you lead them to improved performance, they'll change positions on the matrix.

For starters, get a complete assessment of your team's distribution on the matrix. This view of your team is valuable because some boxes in your portfolio are much more efficient than others. This initial assessment indicates where to focus your efforts to improve their performance. If you can develop your team members such that they move to the more efficient boxes, you improve your

The Leadership Matrix

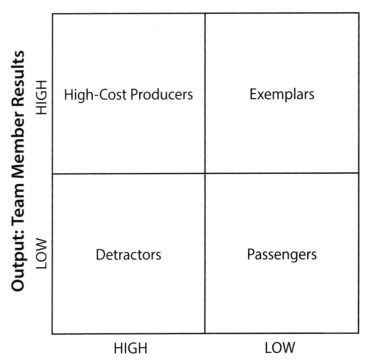

team's efficiency. That should make everyone—you, your team, and your bosses—happier, and will mark you as an effective leader. Not only that—your personal stress levels will decrease as a result. Your improved results will require less time and effort from you to achieve. That will free up your time and energy for other pursuits such as vacation, family time, and your own professional development. Building a team of high performers provides benefits well beyond delivering great results.

How do you get to this state of leading a high-performing team? First you have to figure out what your current team member portfolio looks like. We'll show you how to assess your leadership capital investment in each and every team member and evaluate the resultant output you get from them. This will enable you to place them in the correct boxes of the Leadership Matrix. We'll provide a detailed description of what each behavior type looks like to enable you to correctly categorize your team members. Then we'll offer you a variety of different leadership techniques you can use with each team member to help them all move to a higher-return box.

By way of an example to illustrate how the method works, let's look at the situation of C.J. and Scott and how their leader, Danielle, interacted with them. C.J. moved into a role at corporate headquarters after spending many years in a front-line operations role. He was focused and high-energy, and he understood the operational side of the business in great detail. At first, the work he delivered in his new corporate role was mediocre. He got things done but didn't have all the skills required to deliver high-quality results. Scott had been a field guy at one point but he disliked the long hours and the amount of effort the role required. After several years in the field, he switched to a corporate headquarters role because it seemed to be a better fit with his desired lifestyle. Oddly enough, even though he was in a corporate role, he spent a great deal of his time traveling to visit field operating locations. It seemed as though he was always off doing something related to the operations but no one was quite sure what he was working on. His actual results seemed to be nonexistent.

Danielle knew she'd have to intervene to get both C.J. and Scott to change their behavior. It was clear C.J. should be in the top half of the Leadership Matrix, given his energy and potential. The entire leadership team was confident in his ability to deliver great results. That's why they moved him into the expanded corporate role in the first place. Based on his initial performance, he needed additional guidance to build the skills necessary to deliver those results. Eventually, once he was comfortable in his role, he would need less supervision, but in the short term he needed Danielle to invest more time in him. C.J. was a Detractor—he was taking up a great deal of her time because he wasn't delivering much in terms of results.

As she invested more leadership capital in him, C.J. began delivering better results on a more frequent basis. She spent time teaching him new frameworks, editing his documents, coaching him on how to influence key stakeholders, and helping him prioritize his work. This entailed spending many hours working with C.J. in an effort to improve his skills. During that time, C.J. moved from the Detractor box to the High-Cost Producer box. Eventually Danielle had to spend less and less time helping him grow into his role.

As C.J. became an Exemplar, Danielle backed off. Had she not made this leadership capital investment, C.J. could have remained stuck as a Detractor. He may have become frustrated and could have left the organization. If he didn't choose to leave on his own, his lack of results could have led the management team to move him back to a role of lesser responsibility. If things got bad enough, Danielle could have put him on a formal performance improvement plan and even terminated his employment. Any of those outcomes would have been a tragic loss of a talented team member.

Scott was a Passenger—delivering few results while demanding little supervision and leadership capital investment. Danielle saw his performance issue and increased her expectations of Scott to get him to deliver more results. She asked Scott for regular, measurable updates on his results. She pushed him hard when he failed to deliver them. She was hoping this would move him from being a Passenger to at least being a High-Cost Producer who turned out more results. But Scott continued to avoid work by taking even more frequent, unnecessary trips to the field. Despite Danielle's leadership capital investment, there was only a marginal improvement in Scott's results. He went from being a Passenger who took up little of her time to being a Detractor—delivering few results that came at the expense of a great deal of her time and energy. Scott's continued poor performance left Danielle no choice. She removed him from his position. Once Scott's issue was diagnosed, she knew what she had to do to have any chance of performance improvement. Although the final action Danielle took was a difficult one, it was the right thing to do for the broader organization. Scott was performing below expectations even while consuming excessive amounts of leadership capital. Danielle could better spend that time and energy on other team members who would deliver better results from the increased attention they received from her. These are the types of insights that emerge as you use the Leadership Matrix.

C.J.'s performance was a success story and Scott's performance was more of a failure. Danielle's understanding of their delivery of results, how much leadership capital they needed, and which techniques to use to move them to more efficient boxes enabled her to take appropriate steps to improve performance. Both team members were failing to deliver results but the causes were substantially different. Knowing the difference and leading accordingly is at the heart of the method we're sharing. In both situations, Danielle understood the investment she was making and the results she was getting back. By allocating her leadership capital efficiently, she improved her team's effectiveness.

Part II:
Leader Inputs and Team Member Outputs

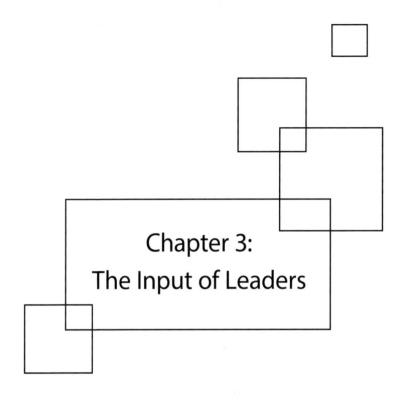

Chapter 3:
The Input of Leaders

Do leaders work, or do they sit back and supervise others? Where you stand on that issue depends upon where you sit in the leader-versus-led relationship. From the bottom up, leading doesn't appear to involve much work. The "real" work happens at the bottom of the organization chart—on the front lines. The higher you go in the hierarchy, you'll see less "real" work and more *talk* about real work.

If you've led people, however, you have a different perspective. Once you've been in a leadership role, you realize leadership doesn't magically happen. It requires skills, expertise, and intangible qualities like gravitas. It takes time and effort to apply those capabilities. A leader's work can be thought of as a range of "leadership services" provided to team members. Providing these services takes time and energy. The same way organizations don't have unlimited financial capital to invest, leaders don't have unlimited time and energy to invest in leading their teams. That dynamic requires leaders to be deliberate in their approach to allocating their leadership capital.

Methods for Allocating Leadership Capital

Because leadership capital is finite, leaders must invest it intelligently. Unfortunately, however, leaders spend their scant financial capital much more carefully than they do their precious leadership capital. Because the financial capital budgeting process is competitive, a great deal of thought is put into decisions about how to allocate funds. However financial budgeting is done in your organization, it's probably one of the most intense decision-making processes you experience.

Compared to the budgeting process, the way that leaders decide how to invest their time and energy in their teams can seem arbitrary. Some leaders spread it evenly across their team members to achieve equality. This "spreading peanut butter on a sandwich" approach may be fair—by using this approach, leaders can avoid being seen as "playing favorites"—but spreading your leadership capital this way isn't strategic. If your organization's Chief Financial Officer recommended that your organization's capital budget be allocated across initiatives and departments in that manner, would he or she be doing a good job? Picture a queue of everyone in your organization outside your CFO's door. They're all asking for money and your CFO starts passing out cash equally, saying, "One for you, one for you..." If you were a company shareholder, would you want to invest more or less of your money with this company, knowing how that capital was being distributed? If you made your personal financial investment choices based on this "peanut butter" approach, you might be well-diversified, but would you get the highest return possible on your investment?

Some leaders allocate their leadership capital by giving more to the loudest requestors. This method is all about achieving peace—the "reactive" approach. Instead of proactively determining where to invest their time and energy, they distribute it on a first come, first served basis. Imagine if your CFO did that with your financial capital. If whoever got to him first was given all the money, would that produce the best return on your capital? Would you make your personal financial investment choices based on which solicitation came in first over the phone or in the mail?

Leaders may allocate their leadership capital where it's easiest to do so—the "path of least resistance" approach. In this case, leaders find it easier to work with certain team members than others, so they spend all their time with a subset of their team. This approach minimizes their stress by limiting their interactions with more difficult team members. That approach is risky. Not only will other team members feel their leader is playing favorites, but the leader isn't getting the return she should for her leadership capital investment. Furthermore, the person who is fun to work with might be the lowest performer on the team. He could be using his social skills to compensate for his performance shortcomings. Go back to being a shareholder: if this company's CFO made financial investment allocation decisions based on whom she personally liked the most, would you feel good? Similarly, would you make your personal investment choices based solely on which stockbroker was the nicest? No. You would want the money invested in areas generating the highest return. The same holds true for your leadership capital.

These three approaches—"spreading peanut butter on a sandwich," "being reactive," and "the path of least resistance"—have benefits, but they're not likely to be the best way to get the most efficient and effective output from the *entire* team.

How are *you* investing your leadership capital in your team members? The notion of investing in areas generating the highest return applies the same way it does in financial investing: If your organization is deciding between investing in one project that will generate a 5-percent return and another that generates a 15-percent return, which do you think it will invest in? To make this simple, assume the risk and the amount invested are the same. The answer is clear. Consider another example: You're investing funds for your personal retirement every month. You're splitting those dollars equally between two funds with the same risk profile. Fund X will return 2 percent per year and Fund Z will return 14 percent per year. In that situation, you'd shift your investment away from Fund X and into Fund Z to achieve a higher return. Your leadership capital works the same way. Determine how much you're investing, where you're investing it, and what return you're receiving. Armed with that knowledge, you can then shift your leadership capital investments into higher-return activities.

Assessing How You're Investing Your Leadership Capital

Placing your team members on the Leadership Matrix requires you to compare where you're investing your leadership capital and the return you receive from those investments in the form of team-member results. The way to conduct this evaluation is through a simple assessment exercise using a grid. The first axis you'll assess in this exercise will be the "input" axis—leadership capital invested. Your investment comes in the form of 12 "leadership services" you provide to your team members. Those services are ways you're investing time, energy, and effort in your team members.

The 12 Leadership Services

The 12 leadership services fall under four categories:

1. **Directing**—Planning, Prioritizing, and Coordinating
2. **Doing**—Deciding, Motivating, and Clearing

3. **Delivering**—Monitoring, Correcting, and Repairing

4. **Developing**—Training, Coaching, and Promoting

For this assessment exercise, create a grid with your team members' names as the columns and the 12 leadership services as the rows. Evaluate all your team members on each leadership service. Assess everyone on the same leadership service at once, versus assessing one individual on all 12 services and then moving onto the next individual. This is a useful way to compare team members on a relative basis for each service. For example, by assessing everyone on the "Deciding" question at the same time, you can perform a relative comparison for how much of that service each team member requires. That comparison will make answering the question easier and will give you more accurate results. When completed, the grid should look like our example on the following page.

For *each* team member, think about whether he or she is requiring you to provide him or her with *too much* of each service—answer *yes* if he is. Fill in those answers on your grid.

Directing

❑ **Planning:** Leaders translate their vision for the organization into team goals and further into individual goals. Think about how much time and energy you invest helping your team members define their individual goals. Some

Leadership Service	Team Member #1	Team Member #2	Team Member #3	Team Member #4
Planning		Yes		
Prioritizing		Yes		
Coordinating	Yes			
Deciding			Yes	
Motivating	Yes	Yes	Yes	Yes
Clearing	Yes			Yes
Monitoring	Yes		Yes	
Correcting	Yes	Yes		
Repairing	Yes		Yes	Yes
Training	Yes		Yes	
Coaching	Yes		Yes	
Promoting			Yes	
TOTAL	8	4	7	3
CATEGORY	HIGH	LOW	HIGH	LOW

people might resist taking responsibility for tangible goals. Others may try to renegotiate goals or ask for more resources to meet them. Your team members should be responsible for determining *how* to achieve their goals. When they come to you for guidance on how to achieve goals without first generating their own ideas, they're consuming leadership capital. If you're spending more time and energy than you should managing this person's goal definition and determining how she'll achieve those goals, answer yes to this question.

❑ **Prioritizing:** Determining priorities is important, but a larger leadership-capital consumer is changing priorities and then reallocating resources accordingly. Team member behaviors can force leaders to reprioritize work and shift resources. If one team member is falling short of delivering on his goals, leaders have to fill the gap that individual has created. If a team member is out sick, the leader has to reassign duties to others—including herself. If someone falls short of a revenue goal, the leader has to get others to deliver that revenue. All these activities require shifting resources and priorities. If this person needs you to cover his shortfalls by reprioritizing work and shifting resources more than he should, answer yes to this question.

❑ **Coordinating:** Leaders provide their team members with broader organizational perspectives and make connections for them. This helps them identify where they have conflicts or synergies with other teams. But your people should be able to make these connections themselves. They should build relationships to advance their initiatives. If they're not, they're consuming too much leadership capital. For example, if you keep reminding a product manager to check with manufacturing before proposing product changes, she's relying on you too much for making connections. If this person requires you to spend more time and energy than you should helping her coordinate with others, answer yes to this question.

Doing

❑ **Deciding:** Leaders make decisions that can't or shouldn't be made by their team members. Some decisions, such as budgeting, are ones only a leader can make fairly. Other decisions require the leader's experience. Leaders have to delegate decision-making authority to team members to empower them to do their jobs. Your team members should differentiate between decisions they escalate to you and ones they should make on their own. Think about how often they ask you to guide their decisions. Are they overly reliant on you for decisions they should be making? Are they trying to push decision-making responsibility back to you? Their indecisiveness consumes your leadership capital. If you're helping this person make decisions he should be making on his own, answer yes to this question.

❑ **Motivating:** Leaders motivate people to do things they don't want to do. However, leaders should expect a certain level of self-motivation from their team members. You shouldn't have to push someone to do her job, and you shouldn't have to debate your requests' validity with her. Even if she always agrees to do the tasks, she's making you spend your leadership capital unnecessarily. She may be training you, consciously or unconsciously, to shy away from assigning her work. It consumes more leadership capital if you decide it's easier to do things yourself or if you assign those tasks to other team members. If you have to drive this person to do her work more than you should, answer yes to this question.

☐ **Clearing:** People run into roadblocks to getting their jobs done. They should be able to overcome some of these obstacles by themselves. Some roadblocks are too challenging for them to clear on their own. In those situations, you can clear those obstacles. You can apply the authority your more senior title affords you and escalate the problem to fix it. But doing so takes time and energy. If you've built up goodwill with someone who can fix the problem, you can spend it by "calling in a favor." Those favors consume leadership capital and deplete the goodwill you've accumulated with others. If you find yourself spending more of your time, energy, or goodwill than you should clearing obstacles for this person, answer yes to this question.

Delivering

- ❑ **Monitoring:** Leaders are responsible for tracking team progress against goals. They do so by checking in with team members to ensure their work is getting done. Review meetings are useful forcing mechanisms for assessing progress; however, some team members aren't good at managing themselves between reviews. Nothing gets done until the moment before they know the boss will ask for it. If you have to check in more frequently with one team member than others, he's requiring more progress tracking and task management from you. Your lack of confidence in his task management generates stress for you. Those interactions consume leadership capital. If you have to manage this team member's tasks more than you should, answer yes to this question.

- ❑ **Correcting:** Team members are responsible for checking their work for completeness and correctness. But nobody's perfect. They can be too close to their work to find every imperfection. Leaders provide a valuable second set of eyes to find errors before they cause problems. If you're finding more mistakes in someone's work than you should, especially if they're repeatedly the same mistakes, she's overly reliant on you for quality checking her work. A particular watch-out is if you find yourself completing her work because it's easier than having her correct it. Your reputation is built upon everything that emerges from your team. Remember—you're investing leadership capital in these correcting activities. If you're spending more time than you should checking, correcting, or completing her work, answer yes to this question.

❑ **Repairing:** Team member errors or omissions can sometimes be overlooked by leaders. The leader may not even get a chance to catch those problems because the team member didn't share his work before acting on it. This team member may deliver acceptable results, but the approach he uses to get those results creates other problems, such as damaging relationships with others. You have a responsibility to ensure these mistakes get corrected, the damage gets handled, and the root cause gets fixed—by you—to prevent the same mistake from happening again. You have to repair damaged relationships caused by your team member's behavior. These repairs can require large leadership-capital investments. If you're spending more time than you should repairing problems caused by this team member, answer yes to this question.

Developing

❑ **Training:** Leaders must teach team members new skills and ensure they receive the training they need to perform their jobs effectively.

Teaching people material they're already expected to know or building their skills in areas that were clearly in the job description they were hired to do is a waste of leadership capital. Re-teaching people the same lessons can be a frustrating experience. When you teach and train your team members, it's not a one-off event. You have to impart the skills and then monitor their application of them to their daily work. You'll need to retrain them until they're competent on the task. If you're teaching this team member material she should already know and training her on skills she should already have, answer yes to this question.

❑ **Coaching:** Team members need their leader's guidance in difficult situations. Leaders provide coaching to get team members through their challenges, build their confidence, and get them past obstacles—both professional and personal. Coaching sessions afford you the opportunity to build a team member's skills in dealing with adversity. These interactions can often be unplanned and require you to reprioritize other tasks you're working on to handle them. The time and energy it takes to coach someone is a great leadership capital investment, but some team members require excessive amounts of such coaching. They constantly come to you with issues they should be able to resolve on their own. If you find this person is overly reliant upon you for coaching, answer yes to this question.

☐ **Promoting:** Leaders advance their team members' careers, position them well in the organization, and build the organization's talent pool. While leaders can make suggestions on a career development plan, it's up to the team member to drive that plan's creation and execution. There are team members who resist career-planning efforts, place the burden of their development on you, and fail to take the steps required to advance their careers. Those behaviors require you to spend leadership capital to get them on the right track, or abandon career-planning efforts for them—which fails to build the organization's talent pool. If your team member wants career advancement but doesn't take ownership for his own development and relies upon you instead, answer yes to this question.

If you've answered yes for everyone on one service, think about how you're setting expectations if everyone is requiring substantial amounts of that service. Your expectations for what you should be doing in that area, on average, may need to be adjusted upward. If you didn't mark anyone a yes on one service, you may need to lower your expectations for that particular service.

When you're done filling out the grid, add the total number of times you answered yes for each team member. Put that total at the bottom of his or her column.

Those scoring a yes on seven or more questions will go in a High Input box on the Leadership Matrix. Those scoring less than seven will go in a Low Input box on the Leadership Matrix. If your rankings put everyone in the High Input box, ask if that's an accurate reflection of the work you do to lead your team. Are you working that much harder than other leaders with similar teams? Are you providing more leadership services than you have in other roles you've had? If you've ranked everyone in the Low Input box, ask if you're working much less than you would expect. If the assignments into the High and Low boxes don't feel right, use your judgment to place team members in the box that feels most appropriate. Leadership isn't formulaic—don't be afraid to apply your best judgment to this assessment process. The resulting grid shows you where you're investing your leadership capital. This exercise gets you halfway to placing your team members on the Leadership Matrix. Next, we'll assess the output each team member delivers, which will complete their placements on the Leadership Matrix.

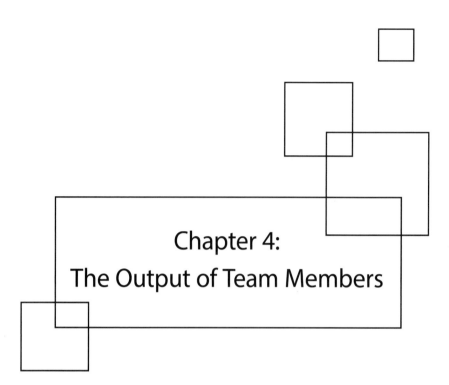

Chapter 4:
The Output of Team Members

Why do you pay your team members? If you asked them, they might answer, "You pay us to work." If you ask office-based workers what "work" means to them, you'll get a list of typical workday activities. They read and write emails. They write reports. They go to meetings and attend conference calls. Those activities sound appropriate enough, but they don't give a complete picture of what "work" means to you.

There are two different definitions of "work" in the dictionary. Your team members likely subscribe to the one that defines "work" as "mental or physical activity as *a means of earning income*; *employment*." Given you're responsible for your team achieving its goals, you probably lean toward the other one, which defines "work" as "activity involving mental or physical effort done *in order to achieve a purpose or result*."

The two definitions are similar in that they revolve around physical or mental activity, but they differ significantly on the purpose of the work. The implication here is that you must hold your team members accountable for the results they achieve—not the activities they perform. That accountability contributes to the collective results your team delivers. Activities your team members think of as "work" are the *inputs* that go into getting the *real* outcome you desire—results that lead you to achieve your goals. Those are the outcomes to assess when placing team members on the Leadership Matrix.

Assessing the Output of Your Team Members

The output question leaders need to focus on is, "Are my team members producing the results I need, given all the investments—pay, equipment, supplies, my time and energy—I'm making in them?" Assess each team member's output—results that contribute to your team goals. To conduct this assessment, create another grid, and make your team members the column headings. The row headings for this grid will be the various types of output generated by those team members. You'll evaluate four elements of team member output:

1. **Quantity:** *What is the quantity of results compared to what is expected or asked of them?*

2. **Quality:** *How is the quality of their final work versus what is expected?*

3. **Timeliness:** *How timely is the work they deliver versus expected deadlines or durations?*

4. **Intangibles:** *To what degree do they improve morale in their immediate team? To what extent do they improve relationships with stakeholders and colleagues outside their immediate team?*

To assess how your team members deliver relative to your expectations, use a simple High, Medium, or Low scale for each of the following questions. Fill in those answers on the grid you've created. Once you've finished answering the assessment questions for all team members, assign a 2 for each "High," a 1 for each "Medium," and a 0 for each "Low." Add those numbers and write the total at the bottom of the team member's column. Those scoring between 6 and 10 make up your High Output box. Those scoring less than 6 make up your Low Output box. When completed, the grid should look like our example on the next page.

Team Member Output	Team Member #1	Team Member #2	Team Member #3	Team Member #4
Quantity of Results	High/2	High/2	High/2	Medium/1
Quality of Results	Medium/1	Medium/1	High/2	Medium/1
Timeliness	Medium/1	High/2	High/2	Medium/1
Morale-Building	Low/0	Medium/1	High/2	Low/0
Relationship-Building	Medium/1	Medium/1	High/2	Low/0
TOTAL	**5**	**7**	**10**	**3**
CATEGORY	**LOW**	**HIGH**	**HIGH**	**LOW**

Output (Team Member Results)

❑ **Quantity.** *What is the quantity of results compared to what is expected or asked of them? (High/Medium/Low)*—Is this person carrying an appropriate workload and producing his share of expected results? If his output can be discretely measured—orders processed, cases handled, and so on—compare his output to his peers' output. If his output isn't measurable, consider the breadth, depth, and complexity of his responsibilities. Does he have a large or small area of responsibility compared to those of his peers? Does he not only contribute to his area of responsibility but also take on additional work? Or does he fall short of expectations and need others to pick up his slack? If his responsibilities are complex, he's likely delivering more output than peers whose areas are simple and similar in size. If this team member is delivering a higher quantity of results than expected, rate him a High, and if he's delivering less than expected, rate him a Low. If he's on par with peers and your expectations, rate him a Medium.

❑ **Quality.** *How is the quality of their final work versus what is expected? (High/Medium/Low)*— You have expectations for how good your team members' products are. Those products can be analyses, presentations, widgets, or customer service phone calls. Their "products" could come in the form of good or bad ideas— bigger and better ideas are higher quality than smaller, less worthwhile ideas. Whatever the products are, you've got a standard for what is or isn't acceptable. Some team members deliver better products than others—so much so that they're invited to work on projects outside their area of responsibility. To determine the quality of their output, look at their work through several lenses. What do customers or key stakeholders say about this person's work? How does the quality of her work compare to her peers' work? How does her quality stack up against what you would produce if you were in her role? Avoid the temptation to base your standards on what you have learned to expect from her. Assess her work against as objective a standard as possible. Focus on her contribution—the work she delivered versus what others contributed to the final product. She shouldn't benefit from someone else doing great work, nor should she be penalized because a teammate performed poorly. If she delivers higher-quality results than expected, rate her a High. If she's delivering lower quality than expected, rate her a Low. If she's on par with peers and your expectations, rate her a Medium.

❑ **Timeliness.** *How timely is the work they deliver versus expected deadlines or durations? (High/ Medium/Low)*—Timeliness is a straightforward characteristic: people either get their work done within the required deadlines or they don't. If this person doesn't have clear deadlines, compare his speed to that of his peers. His speed can impact the quantity of work he delivers. Be sure you don't double-count this aspect of his work. For example, if he works rapidly and turns out a high quantity of products, rate him a High on Quantity and a Medium on Timeliness. Balance your ratings and assign ratings where they're most accurate in terms of what kind of output is delivered. Account for the impacts of the team member's speed on customer satisfaction—customers being either internal or external in nature. If customers are frustrated with this team member's speed, that's a negative. If they're delighted with how quickly this team member gets them what they need, that's a positive. If he delivers results in a timelier manner than expected, rate him a High. If he delivers later or is slower than expectations, rate him a Low. If he's on par with peers and your expectations, rate him a Medium.

❑ **Intangibles (a).** *To what degree do they improve morale in their immediate team? (High/Medium/Low)*—A team member's attitude and corresponding actions can have a large positive or negative impact on team morale. Optimists improve morale while pessimists tear it down. A team member's words can boost the moods of those around her or get others thinking about how much they dislike their work. Her actions—if thoughtful, helpful, and generous—can strengthen team morale. Conversely, selfish and disruptive behaviors can destroy it. Does this team member strengthen or damage team morale? Do people seek to work with her or avoid working with her? If her behaviors strengthen morale and improve the team's mood, rate her a High. If she's harming morale and deflating those around her, rate her a Low.

If she's neither helping nor harming morale in a meaningful way, rate her a Medium.

❏ **Intangibles (b).** *To what extent do they improve relationships with stakeholders and colleagues outside their immediate team? (High/Medium/Low)*—When your team members interact with people outside your team, they either strengthen or weaken the relationships they have, and your team has, with those individuals. Even if they generate great results, if they're unpleasant to work with, they'll detract from your team's reputation. If they're pleasant to work with, they'll strengthen the relationships around them. Their behaviors contribute to your team's brand—positively or negatively. Look at this person through the lens of being your team's ambassador to the rest of the world. How well does this team member build relationships versus what you expect him to do? Do you trust him to represent you to stakeholders outside your team? What kind of feedback do you receive about this team member from stakeholders outside your team? If he is better at building relationships than you would expect, rate him a High. If he's damaging relationships, rate him a Low. If he's on par with peers and your expectations, rate him a Medium.

If you find your rankings put everyone in the High Output box, think about whether that's an accurate reflection of your team and the work they produce. Are they one of the best teams in your organization? Are they one of the best teams you've ever been a part of? Likewise, if you've ranked everyone in the Low Output box, ask yourself if your team is one of the lowest-performing you've seen. If the resulting assignments into High and Low boxes don't feel right, use your judgment to move people around.

This assessment shows you where you're getting the most and least return from your team members. You'll combine these results with the assessment of where you're investing your leadership capital to complete the Leadership Matrix view of your team. Once complete, the Leadership Matrix will give you a roadmap for how to improve team performance—one team member at a time.

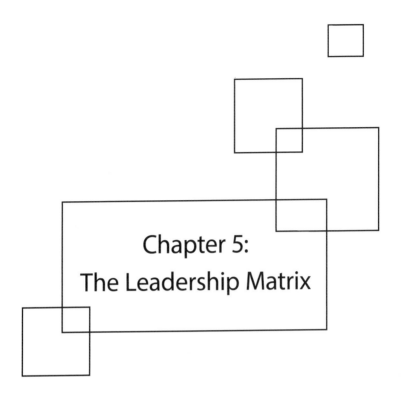

Chapter 5:
The Leadership Matrix

Once you've assessed the leadership capital you're investing in each team member and evaluated the output you're getting from them in return, you can plot their positions on the Leadership Matrix. The Leadership Matrix defines four distinct team-member-behavior profiles that have different leadership needs. Identifying which behavioral patterns each team member is demonstrating helps you determine an appropriate approach for leading them. This approach enables you to make smart choices as to how to invest your time and effort. The Leadership Matrix also gives you a common framework to discuss performance issues with your team members.

Let's plot the team members we evaluated in the previous chapters. Based on those four team-member assessments, their positions on the Leadership Matrix would be as follows:

The Leadership Matrix

Output: Team Member Results	**HIGH**	**Team Member #3** High Input High Output	**Team Member #2** Low Input High Output
	LOW	**Team Member #1** High Input Low Output	**Team Member #4** Low Input Low Output
		HIGH	LOW

Input: Leadership Capital Invested

The Four Primary Behavioral Types

Each box in the Leadership Matrix displays the combination of the effort you're putting into a team member and the results you're getting back from him. Team members demonstrating the behaviors represented in each box require different approaches to leading them efficiently and effectively. To make it easier to determine effective leadership approaches for each box, we've named each one in a manner that describes the behavior demonstrated by team members who plot there.

1. **High Input/Low Output.** Team Member #1 requires a high amount of input from you but generates little output. A team member who is behaving this way is dragging your team down. People exhibiting such behaviors are "Detractors." If everyone on your team operated this way, you'd find yourself investing all your leadership capital in them but not getting adequate results. That would be a frustrating situation for you.

2. **Low Input/Low Output.** Team Member #2 is the opposite of #1—she's generating a high amount of output while requiring a low amount of input from you. People behaving this way are huge drivers of performance. You'd love to have everyone behave the way they do. We call them the "Exemplars." If your team was full of people who behaved this way, you'd be in a wonderful position. With only minimal investment of leadership capital

from you, these team members would deliver outstanding results.

3. **High Input/High Output.** While Team Member #3 is generating a high amount of output, he requires a high amount of input from you to do so. You benefit from having people on your team who behave this way because of the results they deliver, but they burn you out because they consume significant amounts of leadership capital in the process. We refer to them as the "High-Cost Producers." Leading a team full of them would be unsustainable. A team full of people behaving this way could generate great results but at a significant cost. You would run yourself down because you'd have to expend a tremendous amount of your leadership capital helping them generate those results.

4. **Low Input/High Output.** Team Member #4 doesn't require much input from you but she doesn't produce adequate output. People behaving this way are along for the ride with your team. They're not pulling their own weight. We call them "Passengers." If your team only consisted of Passengers, you wouldn't be too busy, given that they don't need you to invest leadership capital in them, but, unfortunately, your team wouldn't be meeting expectations with respect to results either. Although Passengers are easy for you to deal with in the

short term, their behavior isn't sustainable for the long term.

The Leadership Matrix

	HIGH	LOW
HIGH	High-Cost Producers	Exemplars
LOW	Detractors	Passengers

Output: Team Member Results

Input: Leadership Capital Invested

The Eight Behavioral Subtypes

The four primary boxes in the Leadership Matrix are broad behavioral categories. Each box can be split into two subtypes based on the nature of the team member's behavior.

1. **Exemplars** can be categorized based upon their career aspirations. Some Exemplars want their great performance to provide them with a stepping stone to larger roles and responsibilities. These are the "**Rising Stars.**" Other Exemplars are content remaining in their current roles. They're experts and they're satisfied with delivering outstanding results without much interference from their boss. These individuals are the "**Domain Masters.**"

2. **Detractors** are defined by the root cause of their performance issues. Some don't have the skills they need to do their job. These individuals are the "**Square Pegs.**" We call Detractors who have the skills to do the job but lack the will to do it the "**Slackers.**"

3. **High-Cost Producers** break into subtypes based on the kinds of costs they incur. Some get results but at the high cost of damaging team morale and destroying the goodwill you and your team have accrued with others. These individuals are the "**Steamrollers.**" High-Cost Producers who get results but require an inordinate amount of hand-holding from their leader to get them done are the "**Squeaky Wheels.**"

4. **Passenger** subtypes are determined by the kind of output they produce. Some only work to get their paycheck. They expend the bare minimum amount of effort required to keep

getting paid. These are the behaviors of your "**Stowaways**." Other Passengers exert a great deal of energy but they focus on tasks *they* want to do, not tasks *you need them to do*. We refer to Passengers behaving this way as "**Joyriders**."

Once you've placed people on the matrix, step back and ask yourself if their placement makes sense. Leadership requires judgment. You may find situations in which the assessment says their behavior looks like one subtype when your gut says it's another. Use your judgment and place that person in a more appropriate category. One situation in which such moves are likely to occur is with Steamrollers. When you assess their results, they could be turning out work that makes them look like an Exemplar—especially if they don't need your assistance. But if they're ruining relationships and morale in the process of driving results, move them from the Exemplar box into the Steamroller category. The bottom line is use the assessment to guide the initial team-member placement and then use your judgment to finalize their positions on the Leadership Matrix.

Approaches for Leading Each Subtype

Each behavioral subtype has its own leadership needs. While every individual needs to be approached based on his or her unique situation, there are broad approaches you can apply as you lead each of these subtypes.

To lead **Rising Stars**, find them bigger opportunities either on your team or somewhere else in your larger organization. Your efforts should center on **promoting them internally**. Do so through role expansion, providing them developmental opportunities, and giving them the autonomy they've earned. The outcome of this approach should be improved results and retention of a high performer.

Domain Masters need you to recognize and reward their expertise. Don't take them for granted because they don't require a great deal of supervision from you. **Nurture them in place**. Provide them with growth opportunities *they* will find appealing. Don't try to push them into bigger roles they're not interested in pursuing. Your goal with Domain Masters is to ensure they stay happy and continue delivering outstanding results.

Leading **Square Pegs** is about **filling their skill gaps** or helping them find a new role that's better suited for the skills they do have. If you're able to build their skills, expect their results to improve and for them to require less of your assistance in delivering said results.

Slackers need you to **unlock their motivation**. Turning their performance around is about getting them to apply themselves to their work. They have the capabilities. If you can tap into them, they can produce Exemplar-level results.

For **Steamrollers**, you need to **reduce friction** they're causing. The behaviors they're demonstrating while doing their work are generating negative consequences. Build their people skills and improve their ability to influence others so you can continue to get great results from them but with much less "noise" surrounding their efforts.

Because **Squeaky Wheels** consume a great deal of leadership capital, your goal is to **wean them** from their dependence on you. They'll become more independent and continue generating solid results. You'll end up with more leadership capital available to invest in other team members who need it more than the Squeaky Wheel does.

Stowaways need you to **engage** them. You have a responsibility to ensure they're generating their fair share of results. They need to carry their own weight on your team. Your leadership capital investment should drive improved results. At the least, their teammates will see you're holding the Stowaway accountable for not contributing as expected.

Leading **Joyriders** requires you to **refocus** their efforts on doing the jobs they were hired to do. You'll need to stop them from doing the things they *want* to do and train their attention on their core responsibilities. With fewer distractions and more effort directed at their primary goals, they should start giving you better results.

The Leadership Matrix

	High-Cost Producers	Exemplars
HIGH	"Squeaky Wheels": Wean "Steamrollers": Reduce Friction	"Rising Stars": Promote Internally "Domain Masters": Nurture in Place
LOW	**Detractors** "Square Pegs": Fill Skill Gaps "Slackers": Unlock Motivation	**Passengers** "Stowaways": Engage "Joyriders": Refocus
	HIGH	LOW

Output: Team Member Results

Input: Leadership Capital Invested

In the chapters that follow, we explore how to lead these subtypes. We'll provide a thumbnail sketch of what these behaviors look like through a short scenario. These sketches are representative only—no one person demonstrates all subtype behaviors in a textbook manner. We're providing the sketch to give you a good sense for what that subtype's behavior looks like in the workplace. Each thumbnail is followed by detailed explanations of approaches you can use to more effectively lead team members demonstrating those behaviors. Finally, for each subtype we'll provide a real-world example of someone demonstrating those behaviors, and we'll show you how his or her leader applied the leadership approaches we're recommending.

Part III:
Leading Exemplars

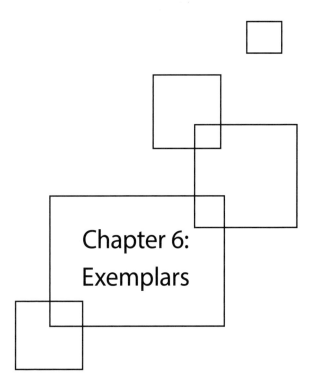

Chapter 6:
Exemplars

Exemplars are the stars of your team who produce great results while requiring little involvement from you. They're the "go to" team members you turn to first when a new problem or opportunity arises. They're so dependable that you often end up giving them more work than you give other team members. You may take them for granted because they're incredibly low maintenance, but if you keep piling on the work and fail to provide an appropriate amount of praise, you may be asking for trouble.

Exemplars are the engines that drive your team's performance. They set a positive tone and good example for others to follow. They raise the bar for performance expectations. You rely on them a great deal to deliver the results your team is responsible for. If their production drops off because they're dissatisfied with how you're leading them, your team's effectiveness is going to worsen. That dynamic reflects poorly on you as the team leader. Exemplars have likely earned fans in other parts of the organization who are interested in following their career. If Exemplars aren't happy with you as their leader, their opinion will affect your reputation across your organization. Finally, Exemplars are a precious resource. If they leave your organization because they aren't satisfied with your leadership, your organization loses and people will question why you let someone that talented get away.

Your first goal with Exemplars is retention. Think about retention broadly. It may mean keeping them happy in their current roles on your team. It may mean moving them to a new role somewhere else in the organization that may be a better place for them to continue to grow. You have two responsibilities with Exemplars: First, advance their careers. Second, retain top talent for your organization. The goal with Exemplars is to guide them to roles within your larger organization that are best suited to unlocking their true potential.

Your second goal for Exemplars is to *decrease* the amount of your leadership capital you're investing in them. Doing so enables you to invest it in team members who could use the additional attention. You can decrease your time and energy investments in your Exemplars because they're self-sufficient. In fact, reducing your investment here will likely increase the results your Exemplars generate. Generally, they thrive with increased autonomy.

There are two types of Exemplars: Rising Stars and Domain Masters. They're defined by how their current role fits their long-term personal career plans. Some Exemplars like their current role but are eager to advance their career. They view their current role as a stage to prove they're ready for the next level. They may be early in their career and they're off to a fast start. They may have come a long way in their career to get to their current role and have come to expect rapid advancement. They may have recently re-entered the workforce in a more junior role than they had before. They're eager to get back to work after having had more advanced positions in the past. They demonstrate a strong desire to return to levels they had previously achieved. Whatever their circumstances, all these people are similar in that they're the "**Rising Stars**" type of Exemplars.

Other Exemplars are completely content with their current job and are happy to stay in it. They're great at it and they love it—or at least love being great at it. They may have been in the same role for many years and enjoy being the best at what they do. Or they may be new to the job but want to stay put for the foreseeable future because they feel they've found their "calling." They may want to stay in their current role because it fits perfectly in their larger life plans. All these individuals are the "**Domain Master**" type of Exemplar.

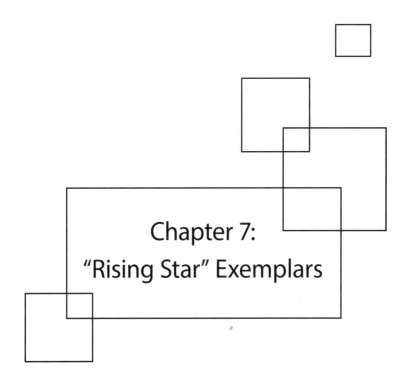

Chapter 7:
"Rising Star" Exemplars

Erin joined your team about a year ago. She came in with many other candidates for a job opening and she impressed you in the interview. She was far and away the best candidate. You knew you would be lucky to get her to join your team. Since her first day of work, she has lived up to the high expectations she set in her interviews. She took over ownership for an important process on your team, and has not only mastered it quickly but has also demonstrated the initiative to improve it. She documented problems with the existing process and used those insights to implement improvements. She reduced the time it takes to deliver her service while improving her output's quality. Since she reduced the time she needs to complete the main job you hired her to do, she's been identifying new projects she can take on to help the team. You find yourself suggesting to other team members that they get Erin's thoughts on how to overcome challenges they're facing.

Erin is the first to offer to fill in when someone else is out of the office, as she views that as a great opportunity to learn about other business areas. She volunteers to lead extracurricular activities for the team too, such as organizing office holiday parties. Erin has been a great addition to the team. You feed off of her enthusiasm and enjoy working with her. If everyone on your team was like Erin, you would have the most amazing team in the company. Looking back, Erin reminds you a bit of you earlier in your career. Okay...maybe more accurately what you *wished* you were like earlier in your career.

Erin is a joy to lead, but she presents you with a big leadership challenge: Her talent makes you realize she could move on to bigger roles. In fact, Erin has made a good impression with your colleagues, and you've heard several of your peers have tried to recruit her away from your team. You haven't asked Erin about any interest she has received from other teams. You wish she would trust you enough to tell you about those offers. "Rising Stars" like Erin are fantastic team members—while you have them.

Approaches for Leading a Rising Star

For Rising Stars, follow an approach of "**Promote Internally**." The word *promote* has two meanings in this situation. No matter how much a Rising Star likes his current role on your team, you have to realize he isn't likely to remain in it for long. He's going to be looking for his next big opportunity soon—if he's not doing so already. It's a huge mistake to be selfish and stifle a Rising Star's aspirations in order to keep him on your team. One of your roles is being a career coach for these team members. Let them know it's all right for them to let you know about their desires to find a new, bigger role. Ask Rising Stars what their career goals are and advise them on what it will take to get there. Prepare them for their next move by helping them acquire the new skills they'll need at the next level. Set a personal goal to get them promoted to a larger role that will take the greatest advantage of their potential for advancing their careers. Creating that trusting environment is essential. You want Rising Stars to know you won't view any desire on their part to leave as a sign of disloyalty.

You owe it to your organization to find roles for Rising Stars that meet their career growth needs. Those roles should be *within your organization*. This is where the word *promote* takes on another meaning: you must not only be *willing* to let a Rising Star go to a new area in your organization, but you must *encourage* them to do so—and facilitate the move. If you tend to hoard talent, talented people, especially Rising Stars, will seek new employment elsewhere. Your efforts toward moving them on to bigger roles are not only good for your organization, but they can pay dividends for you personally too. Being a Rising Star's mentor can be a good thing for your own career, and it can help you build a talented team. Educate Rising Stars about positions available across your organization and get a sense for what types of roles interest them. Network with other leaders in targeted areas across your organization. Advertise your Rising Stars as people who should be candidates for big roles those leaders are looking to fill. Because talent attracts talent, ask Rising Stars to recruit their potential replacements. You can benefit from this approach of finding great new roles for Rising Stars this way: Talented people are often looking for their next great development opportunity, so if you build a reputation for helping talented people come into your organization, grow, and then move on to bigger roles, other high-potential people will notice. Before you know it you'll have a steady stream of high performers knocking on your door asking if you have any open roles on your team. They'll do this because they'll know they can come to your team for developmental opportunities. Not only will you not hold them back, but you'll also guide them to their next great role after your team. This dynamic will make it much easier for you to fill open roles on your team and reduce the amount of effort you expend recruiting. You'll have a more talented candidate pool to choose from because the high performers and Rising Stars from other organizations will be the ones looking to fill the open roles on your team. Once they do join your team, you'll have productive team members delivering great results, which, in turn, makes *your* results look fantastic. While in the short term it hurts to lose a Rising Star to a new role, in the long term it's a great method for building a high-performing team.

Another leadership approach to use with Rising Stars is to acknowledge their reliable performance and reduce your time supervising them. This has two big benefits: First, it frees up leadership capital you can invest in other team members who require more attention. Second, by giving Rising Stars more autonomy, you'll give them more room to build their skills. They'll likely appreciate the increased freedom and trust you're demonstrating you have in them. The best way you can develop a Rising Star's skills is to give her the space to run on her own to learn by doing. Who knows—she might teach you a thing or two.

Case Example: Xing the Rising Star

Xing was a manager at a financial services firm for several years. He came from a consulting background. Despite having no prior operational experience, he took over a small operations team and delivered outstanding results. His team's financial performance exceeded expectations and the team's culture was the envy of Xing's peers. Everyone on the team had a great time working together.

During a major reorganization, Xing was assigned to lead a full business unit. It was a large increase in responsibility for him. His director, Lois, told him she believed he was prepared to tackle the role. Lois knew Xing was more than capable of running the team even though it was five times larger than the last team he led. The two of them agreed upon Xing's goals for the coming year, including the projects and metrics he would deliver. The highest-priority objective was preparing his organization for a regulatory audit. Assembling the required documentation and working with the auditors while running the organization at the same time would be a monumental task. Xing was excited by the challenge.

More important than Lois and Xing's discussion about his goals was their conversation about how they would interact:

Lois said, "I know you're familiar with this role's expectations, Xing. You know, as part of this reorg, I'm now responsible for three other teams in addition to yours. I plan on spending the majority of my time with your peers because, to be candid, they need more guidance than you do. That said, I don't want you to feel like you're forgotten or off on an island all alone."

"I understand," Xing responded. "How about I involve you when I need help figuring something out, need approval for something larger than I'm authorized to decide, or to update you on major milestones. Does that work?"

"I'm okay with that. Remember—the biggest thing I want you focused on is your department's upcoming audit. I'll leave it to you to prioritize your work accordingly."

Xing and Lois reconnected whenever an agreed-upon occasion arose. Lois stayed out of Xing's way and let him run his team. She always knew the status of his projects because he updated her whenever milestones were reached or obstacles were overcome. Xing enjoyed the autonomy. That's not to say he didn't make mistakes. But when he did err, he fixed the problem, learned from it, notified Lois, and moved on to the next task. There were a few times when Xing involved Lois: he needed approval to make a process change, he needed help managing a difficult stakeholder with whom Lois had a great relationship, and he needed her guidance on a new vendor-management strategy. Lois welcomed the opportunities to get involved, and she appreciated Xing's sensitivity to her other time commitments. His self-sufficiency enabled her to spend more time with Xing's peers who were struggling in their new roles.

Xing's team's performance on the audit was exceptional. The auditors noted zero deficiencies in his area, which was the first time in company history there had been no audit findings. Lois not only congratulated Xing and his team on their performance, but she also made sure the entire division knew about their success. She promoted Xing's work to her boss, her peers, and other directors in adjacent divisions. She wanted Xing to be well-positioned for future promotion opportunities that might arise in other departments. Her promotion of Xing's efforts led others to see him as a subject-matter expert on how to succeed at preparing for an audit. He was invited to be on several audit-preparation steering committees in adjacent divisions, and his colleagues sought out his advice when their departments were notified of an impending audit. Lois's promotion efforts put Xing on everyone's radar as a star performer.

When Lois moved on to a new role, she made sure Xing's new manager knew how valuable he was to the organization. She believed Xing was in the top of his cohort and should be next in line for a promotion to director. Before she left for her new role, she discussed this belief with several influential executives to ensure Xing got the look he deserved during future promotion-decision meetings. After a year in his expanded role, Xing was selected to be a director and he continued delivering great results for the organization. Despite several lucrative job offers from other companies, Xing stayed with the organization that had given him great opportunities to grow and the freedom to operate his team autonomously.

Lois's approach to leading Xing made efficient use of her leadership capital. She invested in him as he needed it but otherwise stayed out of his way. She invested that time instead in Xing's colleagues who needed her attention a great deal more than Xing did. Her efforts to promote Xing's capabilities ensured the organization continued to groom him for larger roles. Had Lois not communicated his worth broadly and created opportunities for him, Xing might have accepted a great job offer from another company.

How Rising Stars Impact Your Leadership Capital

When leading Rising Stars, look for opportunities to invest less leadership capital in them. They don't need as much of your involvement as you might believe. Give them room to grow and spend your time with others who need you more. Manage by exception—ask them to involve you when things go wrong, when your input on a decision is required, or when they need your expertise on a problem they can't solve on their own.

When you do invest leadership capital in your Rising Stars, it doesn't always have to be in interactions directly with them. As Lois did, look for situations in which you can influence your Rising Star's career trajectory. Find new roles for him. Share his accomplishments with key stakeholders. Let others know how great he is. These are the investments that retain high performers in your organization even if it means they transfer to another team.

If you lead Rising Stars successfully, they'll continue delivering outstanding results without requiring a great deal of time or effort from you. You owe it to them to create larger opportunities for them. If you do that well, your Rising Stars will take on roles of increasing responsibility. Those roles should be exciting, fulfilling, and advance their careers in a manner they find satisfactory. Although they might be a Squeaky Wheel or even a Square Peg at first, their abilities should enable them to demonstrate Rising Star behaviors in a short period of time. Don't fall into the trap of forgetting to nurture them. Losing a Rising Star to another organization is the biggest risk you face when you lead them.

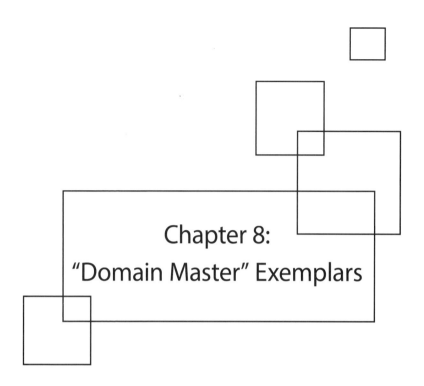

Chapter 8:
"Domain Master" Exemplars

Evan has been on your team ever since you took over your role. When you first met him, he didn't strike you as a superstar. He wasn't a big talker or an attention seeker, but he did project a quiet self-confidence. It didn't take you long to realize he was outstanding at his job. He completed his work flawlessly without causing conflict with other team members or stakeholders. He's a good problem-solver who is able to generate solutions without assistance from you. Despite having broad responsibilities for processes, vendor management, operational exceptions, and technology fixes, Evan knows all those areas inside and out. Whenever new people join the team, they're always directed to him to receive their initial training on how things get done. If a question arises that no one knows the answer to, Evan's phone is the first one that rings.

As does everyone on your team, Evan faces his share of obstacles, but you appreciate the fact that he doesn't create drama in overcoming them. He rarely, if ever, complains about anything or anyone. He never seems to need assistance and he's always the first to offer a helping hand to others. Almost everyone loves working with Evan. The only people who don't are individuals who feel threatened by his outstanding performance. When Evan heard Liz, one of his colleagues, belittling his capabilities, instead of getting mad, Evan offered to work with her to solve a difficult problem he knew she was facing. He dedicated an extensive amount of time to explaining the operations and technology to her. That understanding enabled her to come up with an answer she never would have arrived at on her own. From that day forward, Liz was one of his biggest supporters.

Other managers comment on how great he is. Your peers have even tried to recruit him to their teams. Evan enjoys his job, has been doing it well for years, and seems content to stay in it forever. He has many personal responsibilities outside of work and enjoys the balance he's achieved between his professional and personal lives. He has found his true calling at work and no one does it better than him. He gets the maximum bonus and salary increase every year. Because of his great performance over the years, he earns more total compensation than some people with bigger titles who aren't as highly rated.

You're fortunate the area of expertise he's chosen to focus on happens to be your team. Evan is a perfect example of a **"Domain Master."**

Approaches for Leading a Domain Master

While Domain Masters are a joy to manage, they present unique leadership challenges. Your approach to leading Domain Masters is **"Nurture in Place."** Ensure they feel valued in their current roles so you can continue to get the great results from them you've come to expect. Focus your time on giving Domain Masters appropriate recognition so they feel their work is appreciated. Remove obstacles they face and get them the assistance they need. Reduce the time and effort you spend on traditional supervision to free up leadership capital to invest elsewhere. Your Domain Masters will appreciate your trust and will benefit from the reduced time they need to spend updating you on their work.

Focus the leadership capital you *do* spend on Domain Masters on making sure they have the resources and "air cover" they need to keep delivering great results. Even though they're great performers, it doesn't mean Domain Masters don't experience—or create—conflict. Given their capabilities, they may be responsible for driving large projects and change initiatives, and those assignments aren't without controversy. Your Domain Masters may encounter obstacles they can't overcome on their own. In those situations, they'll need you to take the heat for them when conversations with other senior stake-holders get prickly. You'll need to provide assistance in clearing obstacles. Those are perfect leadership capital investments.

Part of retaining Domain Masters is letting them know how much they're valued. Give them constant feedback letting them know you don't take their hard work for granted. These expressions of gratitude require a range of leadership capital investments. Small investments like taking 10 minutes to write a thank-you note can go a long way. Don't underestimate the impact of small gestures. Take advantage of large opportunities for recognition too. Submitting a Domain Master for a company award can consume a great deal of your time—writing the application, representing him at selection-committee meetings, and lobbying on his behalf are significant commitments to make. Those efforts are worth it on many levels. First, the Domain Master knows how much you value his efforts even if he's not a final winner in such programs. The effort you put into his application alone tells him a great deal about his value. Second, his teammates see your commitment to your people, which increases the respect they afford you. Third, bringing the organization's attention to your department for the great things your team members are doing strengthens people's perceptions of your team and your leadership capabilities.

In terms of new challenges, give Domain Masters options that match their interests. Let them choose from a list of opportunities. They'll gravitate to the ones they're most excited about. The simple act of giving them choice lets them know you respect them and want them to be excited about what they're working on. As far as the types of opportunities to present to them, look for projects or initiatives that will strengthen your organization and challenge the Domain Master's skills at the same time. Recruiting is a great opportunity to involve Domain Masters because talent attracts talent. They'll have a chance to tell outsiders how excited they are about their work, and candidates will hear about your organization from someone who is successful and passionate.

Training and mentoring are other opportunities Domain Masters might find rewarding—especially if you're asking them to develop newer or less-experienced team members. These roles are particularly useful because they let everyone know the Domain Master is outstanding at what she does. It's a great opportunity for her to set a positive example with people outside her own team. Having the Domain Master train others benefits her in the form of increased visibility and respect, while participants in her training learn the subject from a highly qualified instructor and are better able to apply the topics they're learning. Placing the Domain Master in a training or mentoring role tells her you trust her skills and you believe she sets an outstanding example for others.

The combination of helping them succeed, recognizing their success, and offering them exciting new challenges sends a clear signal to Domain Masters that they're valued. Compared to other team members, the investments you make in Domain Masters are smaller and the impact you can expect is large relative to that investment.

Case Example: Mary the Domain Master

Mary's self-sufficiency set her apart from her coworkers. She had a knack for leading investor relations, having done so at several premier organizations. She was intelligent, energetic, meticulous, and hard-working. When investors with big egos—and bigger wallets—needed to be managed, Mary was the first person everyone called.

She enjoyed her role a great deal. Her position was challenging enough to be interesting but not so much so that it was frustrating. Being known for delivering outstanding results on a consistent basis earned her a great deal of flexibility with her boss, Lynn. Her control over her work, her priorities, and her schedule enabled Mary to achieve a perfect balance between her work and personal commitments. When she looked above her on the organization chart, she had no desire whatsoever to move up to the next level. There were too many political games, ridiculous amounts of unnecessary pressure, and an entirely different kind of work that would have taken her away from spending time with people. The greatest worry Mary had about her job was that the executives above her would see fit to promote her and take her away from the work she loved to put her in an administrative role with little outside interaction. All she wanted was to continue to have autonomy and get the recognition she deserved for the results she delivered every day. Lynn knew this about Mary and gave her the space she needed. It was a perfect partnership. Mary was a Domain Master and Lynn knew exactly how to get the most out of her.

When Lynn retired, Mary ended up reporting to Will. The situation became a disaster. Will had a nasty habit of not letting anyone make any decisions without his approval. He was arrogant—he thought his ideas were better than everyone else's because he had a PhD, and he wasn't afraid to let everyone know it. The first rule he put in place was that no communications went out to investors without his approval. Mary was astounded and frustrated at the same time. The sheer volume of communication she had with investors meant Will's rule would now consume the vast majority of her time. Worse, Will was slow to turn things around, and Mary found that by the time he approved a communication, weeks had passed and the message to the investor was no longer relevant.

After several months of this treatment, Mary found herself resenting her job. She stopped suggesting new ideas because Will always shot them down. He questioned every decision she wanted to make. Will even sent communications to investors without telling Mary. Unfortunately, the information he sent was often incorrect. When investors called Mary's office to complain about the incorrect information, she had no idea what they were talking about. It often took her hours to figure out that the root of the problem was the bad information Will had passed along. The few times she confronted Will on such occasions, he denied sending the messages and in two cases he had the audacity to blame Mary for giving him incorrect information in the first place!

Will's bad behavior eventually caught up with him. His boss, Seamus, the division president, saw Mary at headquarters looking dejected. He said, "Hey Mary, why so low? Where's the happy shiny face I'm accustomed to seeing?"

"It's a long story" she said with a sigh.

"I've got time. Let me buy you lunch."

During their meal, Seamus listened to Mary's concerns. He asked what things were like working with Lynn and what was different about working for Will. Mary was careful only to share fact-based observations of events because she knew Seamus would draw his own correct conclusions. After getting a full understanding of Will's dictatorial behavior, Seamus offered an apology and promised Mary he'd rectify the situation. He couldn't afford to lose someone so valuable to the company.

Within a week, Seamus announced a reorganization. Will was moved to a role where he would be an individual contributor. Mary was reassigned to work for Thomas—a leader with a track record of getting the most out of high performers. She couldn't have been happier with the move. Thomas gave her freedom to operate and Mary gave him the great results she had always delivered. He made sure she received the credit she deserved.

Domain Masters like Mary aren't hard to lead. Lynn, Seamus, and Thomas understood that, whereas Will's approach of investing leadership capital where it wasn't needed caused significant problems. Micromanaging and withholding decision rights are signs of an insecure leader who's afraid to let go, trust people, and let others get credit. Insecure leaders feel like they're competing instead of cooperating with their top performers. They have a need to prove why they're the boss. They do so by keeping their top performers "in their place." They tend to overinvest their time and energy where it's not wanted or needed. The result of that behavior is a Domain Master changing positions on the Leadership Matrix and becoming a Slacker—someone who gets a great deal of his boss's time and energy but doesn't return the results he's capable of. The other path Domain Masters take in situations like these is to head out the door to a new opportunity. Seamus understood Will was creating such a situation and he intervened before Mary became a great employee—at another company.

How Domain Masters Impact Your Leadership Capital

Domain Masters are easy to lead—get out of their way and give them the resources they need. Once you diagnose your Domain Masters, you can save time and effort interacting with them and invest in team members who need your attention more. This isn't to say you should ignore Domain Masters. Show them their efforts are appreciated. Share news of their accomplishments with others. Everyone wants to feel appreciated and good at what they do—including Domain Masters.

If you're spending significant amounts of time or energy on a Domain Master, ask yourself why. Are you worried she'll make a mistake? Do you not want her to "show you up" with your boss? Do you think your way of doing things is the *only* way to do things? Understand what's driving your behavior because it's not the Domain

Master who's causing the problems—it's you. Change your behavior by reallocating your time to a Joyrider or a Stowaway—they're the ones who need your attention.

Don't assume a Domain Master doesn't want to advance his career. He might have promotion aspirations that are on hold for personal reasons. He could have a school-aged child he wants to spend more time with, but once college comes, the Domain Master will want to advance. He could want to make more money as he approaches retirement or faces big expenses such as a child's college tuition. In such situations, he can become your next Rising Star.

If you invest too much leadership capital in a Domain Master, you could turn her into a Slacker. She'll get sick of being micro-managed and protest that treatment by dialing back her results. That's a toxic situation. Fix it fast. Resume investing an *appropriate* amount of time and energy in her, given her self-sufficient nature. If you give Domain Masters the autonomy they've earned, expect to see fantastic results.

Part IV:
Leading High-Cost Producers

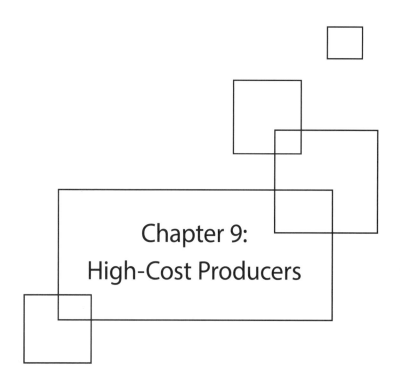

Chapter 9:
High-Cost Producers

High-Cost Producers carry more than their weight in delivering the team's results but incur significant costs in doing so. You don't know how you would fill the gap if they weren't on your team. You're quite dependent on them and you realize it every day. Unfortunately you often have to get them through challenges or clean up messes they've made as they've generated their results. You appreciate the contribution they make to the team but you wish they could do it without creating hassles.

Leading High-Cost Producers requires you to balance changing their disruptive behaviors against negatively affecting the results they deliver. As the "Producer" part of their name suggests, you rely on them to deliver a substantial part of your team's results. If they stop doing so, you'll have a large gap to fill. Because they incur high costs in doing their work, they're weighing your team down from achieving its full potential. They can create problems that affect your team's morale and reputation. Their poor example makes work less fun for you, which then has a similar effect on the rest of the team. Their behaviors can distract you from providing the leadership others on your team need. Changing a High-Cost Producer's behavior can be a springboard to higher team performance. By getting him to be less disruptive, his teammates can spend their time getting their work done instead of complaining about the High-Cost Producer or fixing the problems he causes. You'll be able to dedicate more leadership capital to lower performers who aren't delivering results if you're able to reduce the amount of time you have to spend on the High-Cost Producer's issues.

Your approach to leading High-Cost Producers should be "Cost Reduction." You're going to *reduce* the amount of your leadership capital you're investing in them and change what you're doing with that capital. Wean these team members off of the support they rely on you to provide. Stop figuring out how to overcome their challenges. Teach them how to figure it out for themselves instead. Stop fixing the messes they make and instead get them to change behaviors to prevent those issues from occurring in the first place. You know they have the ability to produce their results without your involvement. By reducing the amount of time and effort you use to support them, you'll force them to build those skills on their own. Like a parent teaching her children to ride a bicycle with training wheels, take precautions at first to make sure they don't hurt themselves. Eventually you can let them go on their own to learn by doing.

There are two types of High-Cost Producers. They're defined by what form the costs they incur take. For some, the resources they require are measurable things like staff, budget, or your time. They frequently seek you out to ask for something, whether by email, phone, or stopping by your desk. Sometimes you wonder if they want nothing more than your attention. These are your **"Squeaky Wheels."** They produce results, but they require constant care from you to do so.

For other High-Cost Producers, the costs are less tangible things, like damage to team morale, relationships, and organizational culture. They get results but they generate frustration with colleagues, peers, and other stakeholders in the wake of doing so. They're so focused on achieving results they may not even realize they're creating problems with others. Maybe they do realize it and don't care about the friction. They view this conflict as a "cost of doing business." Whether they're aware of the damage they're causing or not, you end up spending time repairing the problems they create. These are the **"Steamrollers"** on your team.

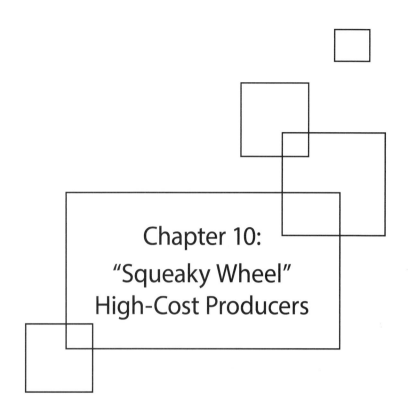

Chapter 10:
"Squeaky Wheel"
High-Cost Producers

Hunter is one of the strongest performers on your team but he presents an interesting set of challenges. He has great experience and expertise. He produces good results you've come to rely upon and consistently gets his work done with the timeliness and quality you expect. You never worry that he won't get his job done, no matter how hard the task. Although you dread the idea of losing him and having to fill the gap his departure would create, you've wondered what it would be like to have someone else in his role. As you've interviewed applicants for other jobs, you've noticed some of them offer as much expertise as Hunter. You can't imagine taking action to switch him out, but getting a fresh face could be nice if he voluntarily moved on at some point.

The main issue with Hunter is that he requires more of your time and energy than anyone else. He delivers what you ask of him but he doesn't demonstrate the foresight to anticipate new opportunities or challenges in his area of responsibility. Perhaps because of his lack of foresight, Hunter doesn't take the initiative to make things happen. If you see a big improvement opportunity in his area, you need to explain it to him and convince him it's worth the effort. When you finally do convince him, he works hard on the idea, but you always have to walk him through it. You wish he'd be more proactive about his own area so you could focus on bigger-picture tasks that affect the rest of your team.

Not only does Hunter need your help to look ahead, but he also requires assistance getting things done. Your regular check-ins with him run long, as he always has more he wants to talk about than time allows. He pops by your desk multiple times a week to let you know about a problem he's having. Sometimes he vents his frustration with other people or complains about how difficult his job is. Other times he needs you to figure out who he should be coordinating with or persuade someone to co-operate with him. He checks with you before he makes a decision—no matter how big or small. Hunter needs frequent confidence boosting and positive feedback. He lets you know as soon as he gets something done or has good news—no matter how small—so he can get your praise. You know providing such motivation is an important part of your job, but you think Hunter is overly reliant upon it. He needs a *daily* pick-me-up from you instead of only getting one periodically, like everyone else on the team. Hunter is your quintessential "Squeaky Wheel."

Approaches for Leading a Squeaky Wheel

Leading Squeaky Wheels requires you to figure out how to "**Wean**" them. You want them to keep delivering the results they've consistently produced, but you need them to do it without leaning too heavily on you to get their work done. Taking back control of the interactions you have with a Squeaky Wheel is how you'll drive his behavioral change.

You may love your open-door policy as a way to stay accessible to your team, but Squeaky Wheels abuse it. Their frequent drop-ins let them control the agenda in their interactions with you. Instead of you being able to focus them on being self-reliant, they're the ones choosing when to meet and what to talk about. You always have to be ready to debate them but you don't know the time or topic of the debate until they show up at your door. Not only is this an inefficient use of your time, but it's also counterproductive to their development. If a Squeaky Wheel knows she can come to you at any time to think for her or solve her problems, she's not going to try to develop those skills herself.

The way to break this habit is to direct your Squeaky Wheels to bring up these issues during their *scheduled* check-ins with you. When they pop in to your office, have them wait to talk about the issue in your next check-in if it isn't urgent. Ask them to summarize their needs in an agenda for your next meeting and insist they send that information to you in advance. Not only will this make you better prepared for the discussion, but forcing Squeaky Wheels to plan ahead also encourages them to be more proactive in thinking about their work. If they try to deviate from the agenda, table the topic and tell them to include it on the agenda for your next meeting. When they lose the instant gratification of you solving their problem on their timeline, they'll be forced to solve problems on their own. Their questions may need to be answered prior to your next meeting, so they'll need to find the answers on their own to meet the deadline. If a problem is urgent, they'll escalate it to you. Your task is discerning the difference between truly urgent and "Squeaky Wheel urgent."

Similarly, redirect their energy spent venting about the difficulty of their job into your existing planning processes. If they complain about being short on staff or budget, tell them they'll have a chance during the next planning cycle to put a compelling case *on paper* so you can compare their needs to competing requests from other parts of your team. Let Squeaky Wheels know that lobbying you isn't a substitute for them putting their best case forward in team planning processes. In fact, tell them it's unwelcome, and then shut the lobbying down. If they're later successful at acquiring resources in the planning process, their confidence in being able to get what they need will increase. If they're unsuccessful, it will teach them to plan better and make more compelling cases in the future. They'll have a better sense for the organization's priorities and can then plan their requests so they align with resource availability and the organization's needs. Forcing them into the planning process also mitigates problems with your other team members. If they're playing by the rules and following your processes but the Squeaky Wheel keeps getting resources outside the process, those other team members will be quite frustrated. They'll feel you're playing favorites. By directing the Squeaky Wheel into the process, you've equalized everyone's access to resources, which is a more effective approach.

When Squeaky Wheels ask for assistance with something they should learn to do on their own, tell them to come back after they've tried a new solution themselves. For example, if they ask you to contact someone to get that person to cooperate with them, tell them they have to try new ways to get the "yes" they're looking for before you'll intervene. If they've been using email to make requests for assistance, insist they talk to the person face-to-face or on the phone before you get involved. The best way to wean Squeaky Wheels is teaching them how to solve their own problems. If you can teach them how to generate more solutions and insist they try them before they involve you, the amount of your time and energy they require will decrease.

Case Example: Regina the Squeaky Wheel

Stepping into an operating role was a big move for Regina. Prior to taking her new job at the bank, she'd been a consultant at a global firm. She had been a high performer there—she was analytical, driven, and got along well with clients. All her consulting work had been on relatively short projects, and only on her last one did she have someone reporting to her. That person was a high performer so he didn't need much supervision or guidance. Regina's new role at the bank was both exciting and intimidating. She was responsible for four associates focused on business improvement analysis projects and had dotted-line responsibility for a call center operations group of 15 people who executed her team's ideas.

Gail hired Regina because of her analytical skills. She knew Regina's capabilities well because Regina had worked for one of Gail's friends, who had nothing but great things to say about her. Regina always found insightful ways to crack problems others couldn't solve. Her ability to identify data patterns and generate solutions was uncanny. This skill was exactly why Gail hired Regina—the area she led required analyzing billions of transactions to understand customer behaviors and launch call center campaigns to change customer habits. Regina knew she was up to the analytical task.

Her role's operational and leadership aspects, however, intimidated Regina. She wasn't sure about this whole leadership thing—let alone leading in a fast-paced operating environment. She found herself questioning her decisions dozens of times before taking action. Although most of her choices were correct and her team generated breakthrough ideas, she did make three high-profile mistakes. Those mistakes could have been avoided had Regina spent less time talking with her team about their analyses and more time thinking through their recommendations' operational impacts, because, although the team's ideas were analytically sound, they failed to account for the training the call center team required to carry out their plan. What frustrated Gail was that the second and third mistakes Regina made were failures for the exact same reason—not thinking through the impact on operations. Regina became hesitant to make decisions and devoted all her time to the number crunching she was more comfortable with. To compensate for her decision-making fears, she began relying on Gail to make decisions for her.

After a few months, Gail noticed Regina was spending a significant amount of time asking for guidance before rolling out ideas. Her inbox became cluttered with advice-seeking emails from Regina. She set up twice-weekly meetings with Gail—one to discuss project decisions and another for coaching on how to lead her direct reports and the operations group. Regina was stopping by Gail's office several times a day to "gut-check an idea." Gail found Regina's behaviors were causing her to neglect other team members because she didn't have the time to spare. Something had to change—and fast!

Gail discussed the situation with Regina:

"I think you and your team are doing amazing work," Gail began. "I'm thrilled with your results since you joined the bank. I know we had a few projects that didn't go as well as we would have liked, but on balance, you're doing a great job. I do need a few things to change though. I'd like you to spend more time thinking things through before bringing them to me."

"But you always have interesting perspectives and bring up issues I haven't thought of."

"That's the point. You haven't thought of them. You're way smarter than I am, Regina. I'd like to see you spend more time asking yourself, 'What am I missing?' or, 'What's Gail going to say I should do?' before you ask for my thoughts. I know if you invest the time, you'll come up with most of the answers we're developing in our time together. I'd like us to move to a 'manage by exception' basis for our meetings. No more regularly scheduled time—we'll only meet when you have an issue you can't solve on your own or if there's a problem that's arisen that I clearly need to be involved with. Can we try that approach?"

"Um, okay. I'm still nervous about making operational decisions though."

"I won't let you fail and I'll always be available for critical decisions. All I want is for you to push your thinking further before you involve me."

Gail saw less of Regina. There were still times when Regina dropped by Gail's office or sent her emails asking for her perspective, but they were less frequent occurrences. Gail also took a different approach to replying. Instead of giving Regina answers, she began asking, "What's my answer going to be?" When Regina answered correctly, Gail would reply, "Well, then, do that. You knew the answer. You don't need to come to me. I trust you. Trust yourself. Your instincts are correct." When Regina went to Gail with difficult questions, they sat down and worked out a plan for Regina to find the answer and report back when she had one. There were occasions when Gail had to provide the answer, but those situations were rare. Eventually, Regina felt more confident in her decision-making abilities. She spent less time seeking Gail's input and instead went to her team for answers. She built a stronger relationship with her operations team to reduce the chances of making more mistakes. Gail was thrilled with Regina's progress. She loved having more time available to get her own work done. She had oiled the Squeaky Wheel on her team and things ran much more smoothly.

How Squeaky Wheels Impact Your Leadership Capital

Squeaky Wheels can consume every spare minute you have, and they'll become overly dependent upon your guidance if you let them. Worse, their consumption of your leadership capital can go unnoticed by you because it feels good when they come to you for guidance. It can make you feel smart. You like being helpful and hate turning away assistance requests. Their requests give you a chance to engage with topics you're familiar with. When you come up with the right answers, your team members are duly impressed. If you're not careful, you can get sucked into this dynamic and spend all your time doing their jobs for them. You can also set yourself up to take the blame if things in their area of responsibility don't work out as they should, because you personally got involved.

Put boundaries around your time. Dictate the situations when your team members should or shouldn't come to you. When you see them being intellectually lazy, push them to come up with the answers on their own or guide them as to where else they can get help. There's nothing wrong with sending them away if they haven't prepared for a meeting or if you believe they're capable of arriving at a solution on their own. The sooner you're able to make them self-sufficient, the faster you'll reclaim your leadership capital to invest elsewhere. You still need to give them support—only at a lower level. Don't leave them foundering. As they begin doing things for themselves, check in with them to ensure they're not struggling. They need to know you're still there to guide them, but they'll now understand that guidance doesn't mean doing their thinking for them. Once you've reduced how much leadership capital they demand from you, they should look more like Domain Masters or Rising stars. You can then invest your newfound time and energy in your lower performers.

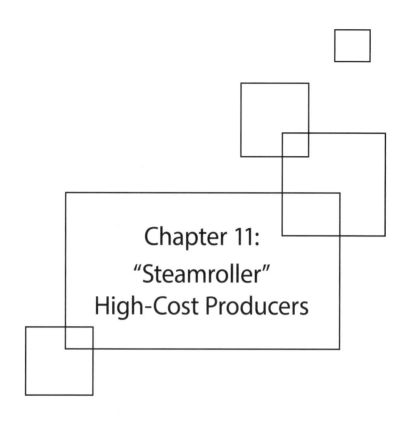

Chapter 11:
"Steamroller"
High-Cost Producers

Heather joined your team a year ago. You hired her after interviewing many qualified candidates. Her résumé was far and away the best you saw. She had advanced quickly through a series of jobs with increasing responsibility. She was amazing in the interview, projecting high levels of competence and confidence. You ended the interview with a "let me convince you why you should take this job" pitch, hoping you could get her to accept the role immediately.

The only warning flag you saw was feedback from Heather's references. They confirmed the glowing results she claimed on her résumé, but you sensed reticence on their part. You heard their answers trail off, leaving an unsaid "but..." hanging at the end. You attributed it to your inner pessimist looking to find a flaw in the outstanding candidate you were hiring.

After Heather started work, you realized your assessment of her competence was right but maybe your inner voice had been correct about the doubts you had. Heather got off to a fast start and proved to be an amazing producer of results. She improved the way work was done by instituting best practices she had learned from prior experiences. However, Heather presented you with unexpected problems. Within a few months, all her peers mentioned she was challenging to work with. They agreed she "knows her stuff" and "gets things done" but they said she was making others unhappy in the process. Heather tended to barrel along and do her work without coordinating with others. There were several miscommunication situations between Heather and her teammates when you had to intervene to smooth things over. Others found Heather unpleasant to work with. What you saw as confidence in her interview came across as arrogance to others. Maybe she didn't realize she was causing conflict—or maybe she did but didn't care. The angst she produced eroded your team's morale and took its toll on the team's performance.

The conflict Heather created generated a great deal of stress for you. You found yourself making excuses for her behavior. You got the sense the frustration your team felt toward Heather began to apply to you as well. Some people thought you were playing favorites by letting her get away with her bad behavior.

Now you face a dilemma. You'd love to continue getting the great results Heather produces without all the trouble that follows in her wake. You know she's talented but you wish she didn't create so many problems for you to clean up. Calling Heather a "Steamroller" is a perfect way to describe her behavior and how others view her.

Approaches for Leading a Steamroller

An effective way to lead Steamrollers is to "**Reduce Friction.**" You want to continue getting great results from them while reducing the toll their actions take on others. Begin by making sure you understand the costs your Steamroller is incurring. Reach out to key stakeholders for feedback about the Steamroller's bad behavior. Ask them to provide you with specific examples of negative situations he's created. Ideally, gather this feedback as part of a regular performance management cycle to avoid drawing unwanted attention to his behavioral shortcomings. Ask feedback providers to explain not only the Steamroller's behavior in terms of his words or actions, but also how that behavior had a negative impact. See if there were damaging effects on operations, personal relationships, or other intangibles like morale and culture. Avoid trying to explain away the Steamroller's behavior and make excuses for it. Gather the right feedback from these examples instead of solving the problems being shared with you.

Next, make sure the Steamroller understands the impact of his behaviors and give him a clear understanding of the problem. See if he's surprised by the feedback.

If so, his main issues could be his empathy and communication skills. Does he understand—and does he care about—how his actions impact others? If he doesn't, get him training and coaching on these skills. Active listening and reading social cues are fundamental skill requirements in the workplace. Set clear goals and deadlines for your Steamroller to apply these skills. Treat those goals just as you would any other expectation you have of him. Hold him accountable by rating him on his progress in demonstrating those skills.

If the Steamroller isn't surprised by the feedback but is focused on sharing his side of the story, you have a different challenge to deal with. Make it clear that these behaviors have negative consequences for others—including you—and that he has to start dealing with those negative consequences too. At minimum, stop fixing the problems he creates. When you solve problems for a Steamroller, you're enabling his bad behaviors because he doesn't have to deal with the problems he causes. Although you have the best of intentions, you're robbing him of the opportunity to learn by doing. A Steamroller needs to exert the effort and feel the pain it requires to fix those problems. If he decides not to change his behaviors, make sure his performance ratings reflect the negative impact he's having on others. If he's unhappy with these ratings and doesn't want to put forth the effort to improve, find him a new role better suited to his attitude. That may mean putting him in a role with less responsibility on another team.

Finally, ensure you factor in the negative impacts a Steamroller has alongside the positive results you note in his performance reviews. If the source of his problems was a lack of awareness or skills in working relationships, provide him with a plan for building those capabilities and then gain his commitment to that plan. If he doesn't care about the negative impacts he's having, spell out the consequences for continuing to demonstrate these behaviors. The severity of these consequences needs to match the magnitude of the impact he's having. Consequences could include withholding bonuses, raises, promotions, and re-assignments. Ultimately his behavior could result in termination of his employment. Steamrollers can destroy your organization's culture if you don't get them to stop behaving badly. You may have glossed over these issues in the past—"that's just how they are"—so be disciplined in the future about giving a balanced rating and meting out consequences. This feedback should make them aware that it's not only important that they deliver results, but that their rating is also a function of *how* they get those results. By forcing Steamrollers to clean up the messes they create, they should learn to avoid causing problems in the first place. Improvements in their behavior will enable you to reduce the amount of leadership capital you're spending repairing the damage they cause.

Case Example: Anthony the Steamroller

Anthony was shocked when he wasn't chosen to take over the team when his boss retired. He had long expected that promotion and knew he was the best qualified. He had been the smartest operations analyst on the team for years and knew the manufacturing plant inside and out. Others praised him for his analytical insights.

When the new boss, Andrea, joined the team, she met with each team member to get to know them and understand their roles. She reviewed their recent performance appraisals. Anthony's results impressed her. The thing that stood out, however, was how sparse the feedback from his teammates was. Although his teammates didn't have the results Anthony did, they did have positive comments about their professionalism, teamwork, and collegiality. And while there were no negative comments in Anthony's peer feedback, there were no positives either.

Within a week, Andrea saw how smart Anthony was. He produced several slick presentations outlining operational improvements worth thousands of dollars of savings. His operational knowledge and his ability to produce the right data was a lifesaver for Andrea on several occasions. With Anthony's insights, she created a strong, positive impression with her boss. She appreciated Anthony's hard work and understood why her predecessor had given him great ratings.

Andrea also realized that the lack of positive feedback from Anthony's peers was understandable. Anthony's name kept coming up in meetings with his teammates. When they had problems getting their work done, Anthony was often the reason. He wouldn't get them the data they needed. When they asked him for information, he would ignore their requests. When they were able to speak with him, he would say he was too busy working on "more important things." Anthony never shared his presentations with others before he shared them with Andrea. The changes he recommended were going to make his colleagues' work more difficult, and he didn't factor that into the savings he was touting. In one case, his idea would have put the organization in serious noncompliance with its labor union agreement, generating bigger costs than his expected savings. Andrea gathered specific examples of Anthony's frustrating behavior, and focused their next meeting on that feedback. After sharing the examples, Andrea asked Anthony for his reaction.

"Yeah, I'm not going to win any popularity contests, but we both know that's not what you pay me for," Anthony replied with a smile.

Andrea knew this was a potential response she would get from him. Anthony was aware of his behavior's impact—he simply didn't care. He had never been *made* to care by his prior managers. She owed it to her team to break that cycle. Anthony's behavior was keeping him from being promoted. Nobody told him this lack of teamwork held him back every time he applied for a bigger role. Andrea felt obligated to tell him.

"It's okay if you don't want to be friends with your teammates, Anthony, but it's not okay that you're not working with them. Your work is suffering by not getting their input. Your promotion opportunities are slim because people think you're not a team player. Your teammates' work is suffering because you won't give them the information they need. The conflict your behavior creates is a source of stress for everyone. I appreciate the results you generate, but your uncooperative behavior is hurting team performance. I'm going to hold you accountable for your behavior. The bad news is that if your teamwork doesn't improve, your next rating will be much lower. If you can get as good at teamwork as you are at analysis, you could be a superstar. Think about how you want to proceed and let me know tomorrow."

Anthony tried to debate the feedback, but Andrea told him they would continue the conversation the next day. After Anthony left her office, Andrea let out a deep breath. Being blunt wasn't her natural style, but she knew it was right for this situation.

A different Anthony showed up the next day. "When I left here yesterday, I was mad," Anthony opened. "I felt like you didn't value my work. I called my last boss to vent to him. His advice surprised me. He said I should thank you. He told me about the bad 'team player' reputation I had unknowingly developed and how it prevented my promotions. So, as unlikely as I thought it would be that I would say this, I want to start by saying thank you."

Anthony and Andrea created a plan for him to build the skills he was missing. He was a quick learner and he hit every agreed-upon milestone. He jumped at Andrea's offer to send him to a teamwork skills workshop and he applied those new skills daily. Within a few months, Anthony was a superstar. Five years later, Andrea and Anthony had not only formed a great working relationship, but they had also become friends. Two promotions later, in fact, Anthony was Andrea's boss.

Whether or not a Steamroller is aware of the negative impacts of his behaviors, the team is suffering. Andrea stepped up to the challenge of delivering tough feedback to a high performer. Anthony's results mattered a great deal to her. Telling him he wasn't meeting expectations could have resulted in a major conflict, but had she not taken action, the team would have continued to suffer. Andrea could have faced an attrition crisis or team in-fighting. By building Anthony's skills and showing him that *how* he got his results mattered as much as the results themselves, Andrea reduced the friction he was causing. She was able to reduce the amount of leadership capital she had to invest to solve the problems Anthony was creating.

How Steamrollers Impact Your Leadership Capital

Steamrollers can be a huge drain on your leadership capital. Their behaviors can cause excessive stress for every team member—including you. You might find yourself dealing with the relationship issues they cause, including team members wanting to transfer and key stakeholders complaining about their interactions with the Steamroller. Your challenge is to get the Steamroller to appreciate the negative effects of her behaviors. This is easier said than done.

Steamrollers struggle to see things from someone else's perspective. They can have a "they should just deal with it" attitude that makes it difficult for them to understand that the root of the problem is how they're treating the other person. Your leadership capital will be consumed by the need to provide the Steamroller with constant feedback and coaching on how to change her behavior. It's a worthwhile investment given the results she delivers. Most Steamrollers are outstanding performers and can learn new skills quickly. By investing your capital in a way that plays to their drive for results, you can see rapid improvement in their behavior.

Making the connection between their behavior and their rating is a powerful technique for getting them to change. List these behavior changes as objectives on their goals for the year. Having them treat fixing their behavior like a business goal enables them to break it down into observable tasks, focus on getting the training or coaching they need, and measure their performance relative to a goal. Use their goal-directed mindset to get them to focus on making the desired changes. Once they do, you'll be able to reduce the amount of leadership capital you're investing in them and they should begin performing more like an Exemplar.

Part V:
Leading Passengers

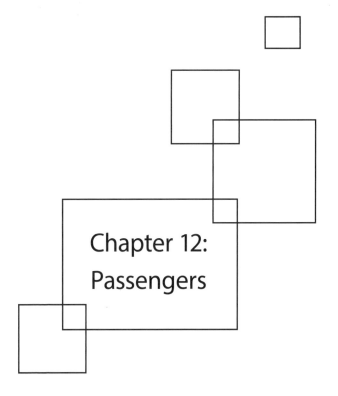

Chapter 12:
Passengers

Passengers fill spaces on your organization chart and their salary consumes a share of your budget. The problem with Passengers is that they're not contributing results proportionate to what it costs to have them on the team. They're not drowning your team, but they aren't pulling their own weight either. They don't create many problems but they do take up a great deal of space. If they were legislators, they would have a steady record of "Present" votes but not leave much else in terms of a legacy of achievement.

Passengers prevent your team from reaching its full potential. They aren't producing what you need but they're taking space on your team that could be filled by a much higher-producing person. Beyond the production issues, Passengers are setting a bad example for what you expect from your team members, which may lower standards and motivation. A Passenger's teammates are usually aware of how little meaningful work he's getting done. They're aware because when that work doesn't get done by the Passenger, it ends up on their desk and their workload increases. Their frustration mounts as they watch the Passenger clock in and out or run off to chase the latest exciting idea. In the meantime, they're slogging away at their desks thinking about how unfair it is that you're not holding the Passenger accountable for doing his fair share of the work. At some point, the Passenger's teammates look for roles with a more equitable balance of work across all team members.

There are two types of Passengers, determined by how engaged the individual is with her job. For some people, the job is a necessary evil they unfortunately have to endure to get a paycheck. They want to engage as little as possible to ensure they don't stop getting that paycheck. These are your "Stowaways." Visibility and accountability are two effective tools for getting a Stowaway to engage and begin delivering her expected results.

For other Passengers, they're engaged in the whole work experience, but they don't necessarily like the work itself. They look for any excuse to pursue other activities they enjoy more than their assigned tasks. These are your "Joyriders." Constant focus, prioritization, and supervision are the techniques you'll use to eliminate distractions that capture the Joyrider's attention. Once you have him focused, delivery of results usually follows.

Your goal with Passengers is to increase the results they produce. In the short term, you're going to **increase your leadership capital investment** in them. Those investments should have three results: First, expect to see an increased amount of output from them. Directing their energy and monitoring their progress focuses their efforts on tasks that matter. Second, your efforts should build their skills to the point that they become High-Cost Producers or even Exemplars. They'll learn how to prioritize, focus, and be task-oriented. Third, by demonstrating that you're going to hold everyone to the same expectations, others on your team will likely increase the results they produce. Feelings of inequality will diminish as the Passenger's teammates stop having to do more than their fair share of the work. Passengers will no longer feel safe trying to slip beneath your radar because they know you'll hold them accountable for failure to produce results.

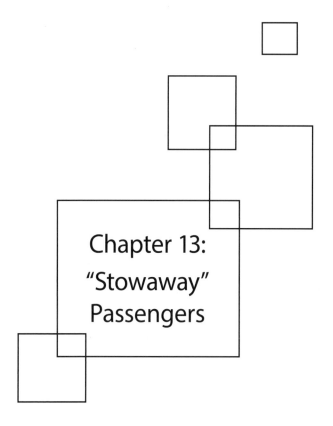

Chapter 13:
"Stowaway"
Passengers

Polly shows up to work. That's about it. If you were asked to name her best quality as a team member, that would be the first thing that would come to your mind—that she's present. If pressed to describe her, you might say, "she never causes any problems." Her biggest strengths are the things she *isn't* and the problems she *doesn't* create. She isn't unpleasant to work with, nor does she burden others with her problems. Your relationship with her is cordial enough but you wouldn't consider it a friendship. She never steps on people's toes or gets in anyone's way. She doesn't complain about work too much or too loudly. She isn't opinionated and she doesn't participate in the office rumor mill. She doesn't speak up much in meetings, nor does she disrupt a meeting's flow. Last month, her colleagues didn't invite her to several department meetings. It wasn't deliberate—they simply forgot she was there. In one-on-one meetings, you struggle to keep a conversation going with her. You end up either driving the entire conversation or sitting in awkward silence after she offers her trademark one-sentence reply. Talking with her is like playing tennis with a wall—you have to do all the work.

The biggest leadership challenge you have with Polly is that you have a hard time pointing to positive contributions she's made to your team's output. You didn't hire her, so you're not sure what her original job responsibilities were. You can't point to any initiative she has driven or to any project you've given her that has been a big success. Nobody thinks about Polly as the go-to person on any topic. When you have to get something done, you don't turn to her because it takes too much of your time and effort to explain what you want and then check on her progress. You either turn to others to do the work or you find it easier to do things yourself. It's almost as if she makes explaining things and following up with her deliberately difficult as a deterrent to you giving her assignments. Polly is a "Stowaway"—she's along for the ride but doesn't want to put in her fair share of the effort to move the organization forward.

Approaches for Leading a Stowaway

Your leadership approach with Stowaways is to "**Engage**" them. They're consuming one of your scarcest resources—a budgeted job slot on your team. Whoever fills that position must deliver meaningful results, but Stowaways rarely live up to that expectation. They're too busy avoiding work and hoping no one notices. Their meager results go undetected because they stay out of sight and don't cause trouble. Eventually their failure to deliver always comes to light—it's only a question of how much damage has been done before anyone notices.

The first step for engaging a Stowaway is to clarify your expectations of his role. You may not have written his job description but you do need to make sure it makes sense. Compare his job description to other roles similar in responsibility and compensation. If the Stowaway's job description looks easier than comparably titled and salaried roles, update the position's responsibilities. Engage your human resources staff at that point, as rewriting a position description can be a sensitive issue. If changing the job description is done poorly, a Stowaway could feel like he's gotten the "bait and switch" treatment relative to the position he originally accepted.

If the Stowaway's job description looks reasonable, your leadership challenge is to hold him accountable. Look at his most recent performance appraisals to see how he's performed relative to what his job description calls for. Reconcile his job description with his goals for the year. Your expectations for a Stowaway may decrease in time based on his lackluster performance—as you become conditioned to what results to expect from him, you may unconsciously lower your expectations to be more in line what you know you *will* get from him rather than what you *should* get from him. That's not a healthy

dynamic. But if you give him low ratings that more accurately reflect his performance, you know it will create
problems for you as the Stowaway will be upset with you.
In some Stowaway cases you might find you avoid managing them because you know it could lead to uncomfortable conversations.

To get a Stowaway producing an acceptable level of
results, increase the time you spend with her and better structure your interactions together. Review her job
description with her to make sure she understands your
expectations. Next, define concrete objectives for her
to achieve in the current performance evaluation cycle.
Those objectives should align with her documented job
expectations. Review these with the Stowaway to ensure she understands them. If you've increased her responsibilities, conduct a formal goal-setting session with
her and get her commitment to delivering on your new
expectations.

Once your Stowaway begins working toward her
new objectives, schedule regular one-on-one meetings
with her to review her progress against those expectations. Unlike previous meetings you may have had with
her, you're going to ask the Stowaway to do most of the
talking. Have her update you on the progress she's made
against agreed-upon expectations. Ensure the Stowaway
knows the purpose of those meetings in advance by sending her the agenda ahead of time. In those meetings, be
disciplined in getting her to do the talking and updating
you. If she doesn't do so with the quality and quantity
of information you think is adequate, let her know she's
not meeting your expectations. If she does start meeting

your expectations, be sure to let her know that too. It's a good idea to communicate that to her in writing. Sending an email summarizing your meeting doesn't take much time and can be well worth the effort. Doing so will not only ensure the Stowaway hears the message, but it will also be a record that you put her on notice. Eventually you may have to manage a Stowaway out of the role and replace her with someone who can deliver as expected. Your paper trail will strengthen your case for removing a Stowaway from her position.

If your Stowaway shows positive traction on her plan, provide appropriate encouragement and feedback. Understand which projects excite her so you can give her similar work in the future. The more you know what she's passionate about, the easier it will be to keep her engaged and turn her performance around.

Case Example: Stacey the Stowaway

Calvin had been leading the travel department for eight years. His team had been there as long as he had. He took great pride in his team's performance and the high customer-satisfaction scores they earned. Despite those high scores, his boss often pushed him to improve several metrics that had historically been stuck at "average" levels. It seemed no matter what he did, Calvin wasn't able to get those scores to increase.

A calendar reminder went off indicating it was time to leave for his boss's Thursday staff meeting. As Calvin got up, he saw the familiar bi-weekly paystub envelope under his door. "Thank goodness it's *almost* Friday," he thought. When he passed Stacey's office, he heard a faint cough come from inside it. Stacey was the one team member who predated his tenure. He thought nothing of her cough and headed to his meeting.

The next morning Calvin noticed Stacey's door was closed. "Stacey called in sick," the intern told him before he asked. "It must be Friday," he added with a smile.

"What's that supposed to mean?" Calvin asked.

The intern offered his analysis. "It's the running joke that Stacey's sick every other Friday. We call it 'paystubitis.' When her paystub arrives on Thursday, she sees she's accrued another sick day and she starts to cough. That's her setup to calling in sick on Friday. It's like clockwork. Pretty clever, too, as she never misses more than one day so she doesn't need a doctor's note. She can be fine on Monday since she's had all weekend to 'recover.'"

Calvin felt the fool for never having noticed this before. Stacey had never given him any problems. She wasn't a standout on his team, but she never caused him any stress and he appreciated that. He did some quick math and realized those alternating Fridays represented 10 percent of Stacey's total paid time. He logged into his management reporting system to confirm the intern's analysis of Stacey's behavior. Unfortunately the data showed a clear absence pattern. Calvin set his next meeting with Stacey to be a full hour and promised to send her an agenda for that meeting a few days in advance so she could prepare.

Based upon his analysis, Calvin summarized all the questions he had into an informal memo to share with Stacey to focus their meeting. He noted:

❑ Stacey's sick leave showed an interesting pattern, with absences every alternating Friday for three years. Her total absences ran at three times the average for his whole team.

❑ Stacey was the biggest user of independent contractor services. Even though demand for travel planning decreased in recent times, Stacey's needs for contractor assistance remained steady.

❑ When she was out sick, Stacey had her incoming travel requests forwarded to the office intern. If the requests were new, the intern would manage the entire trip. If the requests were for changes to trips Stacey had started to book, the intern would take over the rest of the trip. These behaviors came to light during Calvin's subsequent discussion with the intern. The system tracked workload by staff member, but "Intern" was never added as a data field, so all those requests got logged under Stacey by default.

Calvin met with his HR representative to review the memo before he shared it with Stacey. Together, they removed judgment from the list and focused on observed behaviors. Calvin added discussion questions at the end that would serve as the agenda for the meeting. They decided the HR representative should sit in on the meeting as well.

The meeting with Stacey was quite productive. Stacey did most of the talking, laying out all the complicating factors that explained the observations. She promised to do her best to work through them. Within a month, there was a marked change in Stacey's performance. Like anyone, she needed a sick day every once in a while, but the apparent "paystubitis" stopped and she was at work more predictably. With Calvin's close supervision, Stacey weaned herself from contractor support. Calvin was able to cut back his team's need for interns.

Calvin expected those benefits from Stacey's improved behavior, but what surprised him was the impact it had on the rest of his team. He never thought the team had an attitude problem, but he noticed a significant decrease in the complaining he previously saw as normal workplace griping. When he reviewed his stubbornly average metrics like response time and rebooking percentages, he noticed they were increasing from their historic levels. Customer satisfaction scores improved too. For the first time he could remember, Calvin started looking forward to his boss's emails.

Five months later, Stacey announced she landed a government job she had had her eyes on for a long time. Calvin and the team wished her well when they threw her a great going away party.

Stacey's behaviors required Calvin to take drastic action. Involving HR and writing a formal performance plan are big steps, but given the severity of Stacey's Stowaway behaviors, he needed to drive rapid improvement in her performance. To do so, he made a large leadership capital investment hoping to get Stacey to engage with her work. The short-term benefits were clear, and, long-term, even though Stacey left the team, it resulted in a positive impact. Her departure enabled her to pursue a role she was better suited for and Calvin created an opportunity to hire a better performer into the role.

How Stowaways Impact Your Leadership Capital

Stowaways are problematic in that they *don't* cause problems. Their goal is to go unnoticed so you're unaware of how little leadership capital you're investing in them. If they had it their way, you wouldn't invest any time or energy in managing them. You'd leave them to manage themselves. Unfortunately, that approach is a leadership failure.

Once you identify their performance problem, which manifests as a lack of results, you'll need to increase the time and energy you put into leading Stowaways. This comes in the form of more rigorous goal setting, frequent check-ins on their progress, and training them on better ways of getting things done. Breaking their work down and holding them accountable will be frustrating. Those are basic tasks they can be expected to do, but they don't have the desire to do them. That behavior necessitates you doing so for them. Even after they improve, you'll need to monitor your Stowaways to ensure they don't slip back into bad behaviors.

As your Stowaways begin delivering results, they'll look more like Squeaky Wheels or Domain Masters. The Squeaky Wheel behavior occurs because you've made them dependent upon you to break their work down, train them, and give them guidance. This is a natural progression. Don't be discouraged by it. At least now you're getting results from them. Those demanding behaviors can be changed too—review the techniques for weaning them off the need to have you break everything down for them. If you're lucky, a Stowaway can become a Domain Master. Your increased supervision should make them realize they need to engage with their work or the alternative won't be pretty. That engagement is the path toward self-sufficiency. If they begin managing themselves so they don't require your constant intervention, you'll have achieved the best possible outcome—solid results with little leadership capital required.

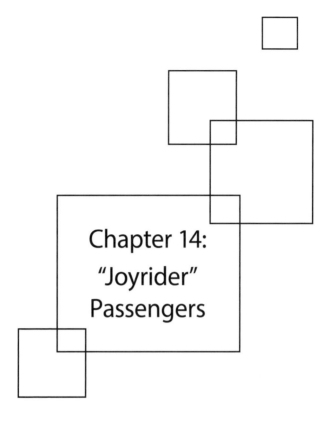

Chapter 14:
"Joyrider" Passengers

Prashant brings tremendous enthusiasm to work every day. He seems to love coming to work. He's always busy with a new project or idea. He's the most social person on your team and he makes sure everyone knows how busy he is. Prashant is vocal in team meetings. He has a perspective on everything going on across the team and he's not afraid to let everyone know what he thinks. He's an unlimited source of ideas for new projects the team can be working on. If the quality of his ideas matched their quantity, he could be a real innovation asset. Unfortunately that's not the case. His ideas aren't bad, but they're not relevant to your team mission or they're not big enough to merit further action. Interestingly enough, his ideas tend to be ones everyone *else* on the team can work on. They rarely have to do with his responsibilities.

The leadership challenge with Prashant is that all his activity is focused on what *he wants* to do, not on what *you need*—and pay—him to do. When he writes his self-appraisal at the end of the year, it's a list as long on "good ideas" as it is short on actual results. It doesn't even resemble the responsibilities listed on his job description. You can't say you weren't aware of all his projects because Prashant frequently communicates his activities. A long time ago you quit debating his ideas as it was a tiring task. The more you said no, the more ideas he would come up with. You realize Prashant learned to take your silence as approval to work on those ideas. His real work does get done—but he's not the one who does it. While he's busy on his extracurricular projects, his teammates take on the extra workload that Prashant doesn't have time for. His teammates have found it's easier for them to do Prashant's work than to argue with him about it. Their choice is to waste their time and energy pushing him to complete his assigned tasks or to do the task themselves because they can't do their own work until Prashant's task is complete. Everyone knows Prashant means well and no one wants to hurt his feelings. They fear he would make it a big issue if people shot down his ideas. Nobody wants to deal with the drama that would ensue. The hallmark of a "Joyrider" like Prashant is the lack of focus on core responsibilities in favor of pursuing work he finds more interesting.

Approaches for Leading a Joyrider

The approach to take with Joyriders to get them to produce the results they were hired to deliver is to **"Refocus"** them. Deliberately or not, Joyriders are masters of avoiding their assigned duties. Make sure the shirking of their responsibilities and their involvement in "extracurricular activities" ends.

Assess why your Joyrider isn't focused on the right things. Perhaps he lacks the knowledge or skills he needs and he's hiding those gaps through distraction. Compare his job description to his résumé. See if there are gaps between the role's requirements and the Joyrider's skills. Ask him if he needs training or coaching to fill skill gaps he might have.

More likely, the problem isn't that the Joyrider is unable to perform his duties but that he doesn't *want* to perform them. His responsibilities are less interesting than the "special projects" he enjoys. Some Joyriders are great at crafting their dream jobs that pay them to do what they want to do, not what you need them to do. When you identify this dynamic, put boundaries around their work and eliminate self-initiated distractions.

When a Joyrider creates a self-directed work environment, be systematic in dismantling it. The reason you're facing this situation is because the Joyrider didn't have structure. She was able to run amok due to a lack of supervision. Create structure and eliminate the possibility of pursuing distractions to correct her behavior. Start with her job description and core responsibilities. Review those with the Joyrider to ensure you have a common understanding of what she's expected to deliver.

Have her inventory where she spends her time and map her time allocations to her expected results. If she's said something is her top priority but she's spending little time on it, have her explain the logic behind that mismatch. There might be an acceptable reason for the inconsistency—maybe the project is winding down so she's spending her time on her next big project. More often than not, however, there's not a good explanation. This insight should focus the Joyrider's efforts where they will deliver the results you expect.

For activities Joyriders say *are* focused on their core responsibilities, get a clear explanation of what the Joyrider does versus what others in similar roles do. Discreetly validate the Joyrider's view of all the work he does. Ask his colleagues and key stakeholders if the activities the Joyrider is claiming he's performing are actually getting done. Assess how his actual workload compares to that of his peers. Keep the Joyrider's workload equal to the workload of your other team members. For the Joyrider's extracurricular activities that aren't mapped to their responsibilities, make him justify those activities. Have him explain the benefits of those activities and who the "customer" is. Have him cease work on ones he can't make a compelling case for. Even for activities that have merit, have him cease work on those too. Explore reassigning those tasks to someone else to see if others value them. If nobody else is excited about those tasks and no stakeholders are clamoring for your team to complete those activities, then they're probably not worth doing.

After you get a Joyrider focused on her core responsibilities, monitor her in a systematic way. If you don't, the Joyrider may once again abandon her core activities and pursue more interesting shiny objects. Check in regularly with your Joyrider to have her update you on her results. Add structure to keep her focused on her core responsibilities. Define the agenda for her and don't let her redirect check-ins off topic. If she brings up new ideas, tell her she can propose they be added to a future meeting's agenda. That new idea should *only* make it onto the agenda if the Joyrider can make a compelling case for discussing it. Be wary of her using "putting it on the agenda" as an excuse to work on it anyway.

If you can't get a Joyrider redirected in a reasonable timeframe, change your approach and manage him out of his position so you can put someone in it who will deliver on your expectations. Work with him to find a new role that has more of the type of activities he prefers to do. For example, if he's always pursuing new social media ideas but you run a finance team, reach out to your digital marketing team to see if there's an open slot the Joyrider is better suited for. If you can't find such a position in your organization, put the Joyrider on a formal performance improvement plan. Utilize your organization's performance-management processes to remove him from his role if he doesn't improve.

Case Example: Lars the Joyrider

Lars was thrilled with how the office holiday party went. He had spent countless hours planning it. Everyone had a great time. He knew he could be a professional party planner if he ever left his project management job.

Lars's boss, Arturo, stopped by for the end of the party. The end of the year wasn't only the holiday season—it was also time to close out annual advertising sales reports. This year would be tough as the company had made several recent acquisitions. They had to consolidate information from multiple systems that used different data definitions. Arturo was in a high-pressure situation so he put the team on an "all-hands" status.

Arturo started his team's daily huddle with project updates. He loved the huddle. Every task was summarized on a Post-It note with clear ownership defined. By the end of the meeting, only two Post-It notes remained to be discussed. "Lars is cleaning up from the party. We'll have him update us tomorrow," someone offered.

When Arturo returned to his office, he saw an email from Lars labeled "Update." Unfortunately it wasn't the project update he expected. It was a long recap of the party, thanking everyone for their contributions. He had included party pictures and a hyperlink to a survey asking people to rate "Lars's Holiday Extravaganza." Lars popped into Arturo's office and asked, "What do you think?" He was clearly proud of his work.

The party was not the top item on Arturo's mind. "Actually Lars, we missed you at the huddle. How are your two items going?"

"Honestly, I haven't had time to think about them. That party was more work than I expected. Besides, Neeraj and Ming said they'd cover those. Don't worry."

Lars's response struck a nerve with Arturo. He took a breath before replying. "The party was great," he began. "I appreciate your hard work. What would make my day would be getting a status on your year-end project items. Can you get me that information tomorrow?"

"Didn't you like the party? I worked really hard on it."

"Yes, Lars. I appreciate you volunteering to do that. Now let's focus on your projects. I look forward to your update tomorrow."

The next day, Arturo got down to business. "Okay, Lars. Let's dive in." He expected Lars to pull out reports, but instead he started talking. After discussing how many late nights he'd worked, Arturo stopped him and asked for the project list. Lars said he was only planning on updating him verbally.

"Actually, Lars, let's make sure we write this down so we don't miss anything. Write your project list on my whiteboard so we're on the same page," Arturo said, as he handed him a marker.

Lars wrote down 12 vague project descriptions. The discussion went downhill fast. When Lars explained a project, Arturo had to ask what it was, who asked for it, and when it was due. Much to his surprise, Lars consistently said *Arturo* was the project sponsor. Arturo vaguely remembered a short conversation about each project. Yes, he remembered saying a team offsite was a good idea, but Arturo didn't know Lars was researching potential locations. Yes, Lars asked if a training course would be useful for the team, but Arturo didn't know he was assessing vendors.

When Lars finished, Arturo asked, "Where are your two year-end closing project items?"

"Oh, I told you Neeraj and Ming said they'd do those," Lars said with a smile.

"Lars, we need to focus on that project *exclusively* in the coming weeks. Put all your other projects on hold. You're not to work on them until I sign off *in writing* on restarting them. Don't start any new projects unless I approve in writing. Take back the two items you gave to Neeraj and Ming. You're only to work on those two items until they're completed. I'll send you a summary of this discussion via email to ensure we're on the same page."

For several weeks, Arturo checked in with Lars frequently and focused his efforts on his two priorities. It was a tedious process, but Arturo's high involvement ensured Lars completed his projects.

After the year closed successfully, Arturo conducted a review with Lars and asked him how he thought his projects went. He told Lars he was going to have to be more autonomous and handle more than two projects at once to meet his job expectations.

"To be honest, I hated it," Lars said. "If all my projects are like that, I'll be pretty unhappy." Arturo told Lars about a time in his career when he took the wrong job and was miserable at it until his boss found him a new role where he thrived. Lars confided that he'd already decided to look for a new job and wondered how Arturo could enable his transition.

A year later, Arturo received a large promotion, so he threw a celebration at his home. He hired a successful party planner named Lars.

Arturo's approach to managing Lars's Joyrider tendencies was painful for both of them but it was effective. Refocusing someone with boundless energy can be difficult. Arturo provided constant supervision and defined specific deliverables. Documenting expectations about what Lars would and wouldn't work on went a long way toward getting him to deliver the desired results. Ultimately, Lars realized his interests were causing his Joyrider tendencies, so he decided to follow a different career path better aligned with his passions. By enabling him to do so, Arturo opened a role on his team for someone whose skills were a better fit for the position.

How Joyriders Impact Your Leadership Capital

Joyriders often appear not to need your attention. They're always busy and appear to be productive. Once you realize you're not getting the results they're accountable for, they can consume a substantial amount of your leadership capital. Refocusing a Joyrider who only wants to work on other things is a daily challenge. It requires specificity not only about what she *should* do but also work she *shouldn't* do. These investments of your time and energy can be frustrating but they're worth it.

Refocusing a Joyrider on more productive tasks can yield immediate results. She's engaged in her work, after all, and she wants to be a valued contributor to team efforts. Channeling that energy into productive pursuits can move her from being a Joyrider to becoming a High-Cost Producer. As she makes this shift, she'll behave like a Squeaky Wheel. She may not come to you constantly for guidance, so you'll need to go to her to ensure she stays focused and continues delivering results.

If you don't invest additional leadership capital in Joyriders, you're wasting valuable resources. They're taking up a spot on your team but they're not returning any results to the organization. Their lack of focus can cause resentment among their peers who wonder why the Joyrider gets to work on anything he wants while the rest of the team has to fulfill the Joyrider's real commitments. Don't underestimate the negative effects Joyriders can have on morale. While they're engaged and happy, their colleagues are working harder, and they can feel as though you're playing favorites. This can result in attrition and lower productivity. Invest your time and energy in fixing a Joyrider situation before it spirals out of control.

Part VI:
Leading Detractors

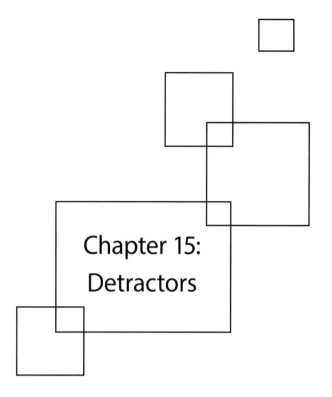

Chapter 15:
Detractors

It's obvious to everyone that Detractors aren't getting their job done. They occupy a valuable slot on your team, but don't produce the commensurate results. They create a negative drag because they require leadership capital that could yield better results if invested elsewhere. When a mess happens with your team, chances are the Detractor is involved. Your Detractors consume a disproportionate amount of your time and create excessive stress.

Detractors make your team worse every day. Not only are they underperforming, but they're also making everyone else's jobs more difficult and less fun. Addressing

Detractors aggressively is hard work that can be unpleasant, but it's necessary. Left unchecked, they can sink your whole team—and even your career.

Detractors require rapid improvement, redeployment, or removal. Their behavior affects you negatively because you're being worn down by all the stress they create. If Detractors don't improve, they're eventually going to fail professionally. They're one corporate reorganization or layoff away from being unemployed. They feel the stress associated with their poor performance too. Similar to others on your team, they want to feel the sense of self-worth that comes along with being good at what they do.

In the short term—two to three months—**increase your leadership capital investment** in your Detractors to improve their performance or move them to a different role. Create a sense of urgency for Detractors. Make them understand their current performance isn't acceptable. Detractors may have been in their situations for years, because many managers would rather avoid the problem for fear of creating uncomfortable interactions. They're called "difficult conversations" for a reason! You owe it to the Detractor and the organization to fix the problem on your watch and not pass it along to the next manager. You have an obligation to the Detractor to tell him the truth about his performance. Do everything you can to improve his performance. Put yourself in his position—would you rather get a warning shot about your poor performance now, or would you prefer to be unexpectedly laid off because you weren't meeting expectations? Leaders must deliver difficult messages, and do so sooner rather than later.

Personnel role changes are frequent. Weak managers may calculate that fixing a Detractor's situation will require significant short-term effort, but fail to realize the benefit of her improved performance is a long-term payoff—that payoff may even come after the manager has moved to another team. The rational thing for a weak manager to do is to not invest in the Detractor because the manager gets no benefit from doing so. Short-term thinking like this is weak leadership. Strong leaders know better. You have a responsibility to think long-term. If the organization will benefit from you investing leadership capital in improving a Detractor, it doesn't matter if that improvement happens while she reports to you or not. The organization is investing in you by paying your salary. The return you provide is building a better team than the one you were assigned. The reason you're dealing with a Detractor might be because the leader before you didn't invest in fixing the problem. Now you're the one stuck with the challenge. Do you want to have a similar reputation for passing problems along? Of course not!

There are two types of Detractors, defined by their poor performance's root cause. For some, they lack the skills to get the job done. They may have landed in a job above their capabilities or they've been reorganized into a role for which they're not well-suited. They may have picked the wrong role for their particular skill set. These are your **"Square Pegs"**—there's a disconnect between their capabilities and the role they fill. Other Detractors may have the skills for the job but lack the will to apply themselves to deliver results. These are your **"Slackers"**—they're in a job they're qualified to do but they don't seem to want to do it.

When faced with a Detractor, realize you'll make large leadership capital investments in turning his performance around. Building skills and unlocking motivation are two key leadership responsibilities. Great leaders demonstrate these competencies in an exemplary way, and Detractors provide perfect opportunities for leaders to practice these skills.

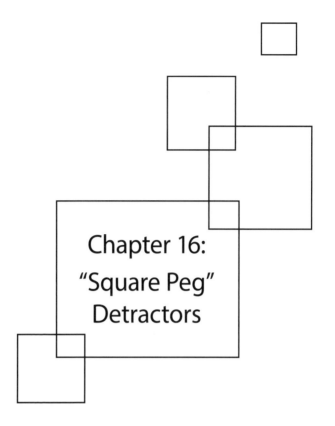

Chapter 16: "Square Peg" Detractors

Dawn somehow manages to consume 90 percent of your time and energy. You have to constantly show her how to do her job, spelling out exactly what she needs to do and how she needs to do it. You like teaching people new skills, but the problem with Dawn is you have to show her the same things repeatedly. After you've explained what she needs to do, you've learned you can't trust that she will do it correctly. You have to constantly check on her progress. When she does finish her work, you have to double-check everything. From typos to calculation errors to important data omissions, your reviews always catch errors that need to be fixed. Her mistakes are easy to spot, and you often end up correcting them yourself. You know doing so will be easier than pointing out the mistakes to her and showing her how to fix them.

Other people avoid working with Dawn whenever possible. This creates an entirely different set of problems for you. While she struggles to keep up with her job, Dawn is territorial and doesn't want anyone else "in her business" because she's insecure about letting other people look more knowledgeable about her area than she is. She's been in her role for a long time and feels like she's the only person who knows how the job should be done. She often asks you for more staff or budget, but that's the only "help" she's willing to accept.

Dawn complains to you when her peers try to go around her. Because you understand why her teammates circumvent her, it's hard for you to discipline them for doing so. Obviously there's a reason they're avoiding working with her. You can't argue with the fact that her teammates get things done when they take this kind of initiative. Dawn's performance has been poor for so long that her peers go around her whenever possible. Her name comes up as a recurring topic in your one-on-one conversations with other team members. Those mentions take the form of complaints about how Dawn is slowing the team down because she's making mistakes or she's making it difficult for people to get their work done. She's the only member of your team who is talked about this way. It's painfully obvious that Dawn lacks the skills to do her job well. You know she's trying her best but it's not working out. When you look at her performance and the leadership capital you're investing in her, it's clear Dawn is a "Square Peg."

Approaches for Leading a Square Peg

Your approach to leading Square Pegs should be "**Fill Skill Gaps**." Change their performance by having them improve or by finding them another job better suited to their skill set. You can do so two ways—either improve the Square Peg's skills or replace him with someone who has the skills required. Sometimes it's not a Square Peg's fault he's in a role ill-suited for his skills. A prior manager may have done a poor job assigning him the right kind of work. Perhaps a reorganization thrust him into a role beyond his capabilities. Maybe he needed to attend training but budget cuts delayed it. Whatever the reason, there's a capability gap you must fill.

Tell the Square Peg his current performance is unacceptable. If he hasn't been told by you or previous leaders that he isn't meeting expectations, the time is now to make sure he knows he's falling short. Plan a performance review conversation. Get guidance from HR before that meeting. Gather feedback from peers and stakeholders to make sure your assessment of the Square Peg's performance is well-grounded. Document your expectations by reviewing the job description and the role's performance appraisal criteria. Gather the Square Peg's past appraisals to summarize his performance history. Complete a new appraisal that describes his current performance. Include tangible examples to give him a complete picture of how he's doing. Include positive feedback as well so you're providing a comprehensive perspective.

Once you have agreement on his current performance, show your Square Peg there's a path to improvement. Discuss with him why those gaps exist. There could be many reasons for underperformance. Has he received the required training? Does he have the resources he needs? Has he received sufficient coaching? Confirm what the gaps are *and* why they exist. That knowledge forms the basis of your improvement plan. Agree upon the highest-priority gaps to fill and behaviors to change. This plan will provide both of you with a sense for what's required to make those improvements—things like training, coaching, studying, or practice. Set a deadline for the situation to change, either by the Square Peg improving or by you moving him out of the role. This doesn't have to be a threat, but he should appreciate the gravity of the situation. To reduce the shock that could accompany that news, let him know you'll work with him to find a role more appropriate for his skills if need be.

Shortly after your first meeting ask him how he wants to proceed. Does he want to do the difficult work to improve? Or would he rather find a new role better suited to his skills? In this situation, you're serving as his career coach. Understand his career aspirations so you can show him how to achieve that goal. If he wants to stay in the role, help him do so. Invest your time and other resources, such as training budget, coaching, and continuing education funding, to turn his performance around. If he doesn't believe he'll be able to meet your expectations, even with all the investments you're willing to make, be prepared to discuss what his next role could be. If he wants to move on, guide him forward. Steer him to a more appropriate career. Identify possible roles he would succeed at. Ideally you'll be able to give him several role suggestions within your organization. He could be a great talent you're able to unlock by moving him to a different function or business unit. That move saves your organization time, recruiting costs, and effort. The person is likely already a cultural fit—it's only a matter of finding a role that's well-matched with his capabilities. Whichever way the situation goes, support the Square Peg as he navigates this stressful situation. At the same time, make plans for how to manage him out of his role and replace him if he doesn't improve.

If you choose to manage a Square Peg out of his role, involve HR. Ensure you have the required documentation to take action. If possible, suggest to the Square Peg that he should consider a role change. Arrange for him to leave voluntarily if possible. It preserves his dignity, gives him flexibility, reduces the pressure related to the change, and keeps the separation amicable. He may be willing to stay to train his replacement to ensure a smooth transition. Managing someone out of a role is extremely difficult, so don't jump straight to the most confrontational approach. The more the Square Peg sees a departure as his choice, the easier the move will be.

Case Example: Felicia the Square Peg

No one could lead a major IT project like Felicia could. She knew the company's systems in great detail.

Not only did she understand the technology infrastructure, but she also grasped the business processes it supported. In the last year alone, Felicia completed four multimillion-dollar technology projects including an overhaul of the company's primary transaction engine.

When the time came to select new leaders for three business units, Felicia's name was near the top of the list. The CIO endorsed her transition into a "business" role even though he'd lose one of his Rising Stars if she moved. The leadership team was confident Felicia would be as successful in a business-unit role as she was leading technology projects. When she was named as the business unit's new leader, everyone in the organization was excited—except Felicia. Although she knew it was a great opportunity, she worried she might not have the business knowledge required for the role.

Felicia's first projects were reorganizing her team and submitting a budget. Neither went smoothly. Her proposed organization chart was fraught with problems. People were placed in roles beyond their capabilities, several roles had outdated job descriptions, and high performers were buried deep in the organization. Micah—Felicia's boss—was as surprised as he was displeased. He didn't understand how she could miss such obvious problems. He was even less pleased with her budget. Numbers didn't add up, forecasts were aggressive, assumptions weren't documented, and the financial plan fell short of the goals Micah had set for her. It was time for an intervention.

"Felicia, I don't understand what's going on," Micah said. "Your org chart proposal doesn't make sense. Your budget is inaccurate and won't meet your goals."

"I'm sorry, Micah. I'm doing the best I can." Micah knew this was true. Felicia worked harder than all three of his other direct reports—combined. He told her to re-submit her proposals as soon as possible.

After reviewing Felicia's revisions, Micah was surprised to see little improvement. He stopped by her office to discuss the issue. "I reviewed your new proposals and they still don't make sense. I'm not sure what's going on, Felicia. How can I help?"

"This is hard for me to say but I've never created an org chart, nor have I ever submitted a budget—let alone built one from scratch. In my IT role, project teams were always selected before I was assigned and the budget was scoped by Finance. I've never been trained in these areas. This is my first attempt at both. I'm embarrassed that I've gone this far in my career but I've never learned these basic skills."

"There's nothing to be embarrassed about. I'm the one who should feel bad. I made assumptions about your experience and put you in a tough position. I apologize for that. Let's finish the org chart and budget together. Then we'll figure out how we can get you the training you need."

Micah spent several days in Felicia's office working on the org chart and budget. They discussed the content of those items and he shared his thoughts on how to build them. He asked his Finance Manager to give

Felicia training on the budgeting process and to be "on call" if she needed assistance. He had his HR representative walk Felicia through the processes for creating job descriptions, performing succession planning, and managing high-potential associates. Eventually Felicia completed the org chart and budget. They weren't great but they were passable.

Felicia worked hard to acquire new skills that year. Running a business unit day to day was entirely different than the project-based work she was used to. Even though she learned a great deal due to Micah's substantial investment of time training her, she still struggled to deliver results. During her year-end review, Felicia asked Micah for assistance.

"I've enjoyed running the business unit. I've learned more than I ever imagined I could. That said, I'm disappointed in the results I delivered, and I know you are too. This experience has been great and frustrating at the same time. I don't think an operating role is a good fit for me. I do much better with running large projects. I'd like to move back to a role doing that. Will you support me in making that transition?"

"I hate to lose you, Felicia. You're the hardest worker I know, and I respect the effort you put into this role. Although your departure will create a big hole, it's more important to me that you're successful. Of course I'll support your transition. The skills you learned in this role will make you an even stronger IT program leader."

Felicia's move to an unfamiliar role had shifted her from being a Rising Star to performing like a Square Peg.

Her leaders could have done a better job of assessing her skills before putting her in the new role. Fortunately she was mature enough to highlight the gap and ask for assistance. Micah made appropriate leadership capital investments to fill her skill gaps, and although this investment improved her results, she wasn't a great fit for the role long-term. Changing her role was a good decision for everyone. Felicia returned to being a Rising Star. Micah filled the skill gaps related to the role by replacing Felicia. The organization benefitted because it retained someone with outstanding talents that needed to be better deployed in a role more suited to her skills.

How Square Pegs Impact Your Leadership Capital

Square pegs are painful to have on your team, but once you recognize their situation, leading them can be rewarding. Their lack of results stems from not having skills—but skills can be acquired. At first you'll invest a great deal of leadership capital in a Square Peg. Whether it's time you spend training or coaching her, making a case to send her to training, or finding her a mentor, you'll expend effort filling her skill gaps. You'll spend time and energy giving her feedback on her performance and skill-building efforts. When you ask her to invest her energy in building her own capabilities, you owe it to her to invest a similar amount in guiding her through that growth.

This growth period will be an uncomfortable time for Square Pegs. They may lack confidence in their capabilities. They'll experience frustration and require encouragement when they're unsuccessful in applying one of their new skills. When they fail, they'll need to know you understand that they are trying to improve and you're not going to punish them for failing to meet heightened expectations immediately. Supporting them through this transition is a worthwhile leadership capital investment.

If they're able to build their skills, their results should improve. Progress could be slow at first, but as they master their new skills, their performance improvement will accelerate. As it does, you could see them progress from being Square Pegs to being Squeaky Wheels. They may check in with you frequently to get guidance and motivation as they become comfortable with their new skills. Once they're confident in those new abilities, you'll be able to invest less leadership capital in them. Hopefully that autonomy paves the way for them to become Exemplars who deliver results that require less coaching from you.

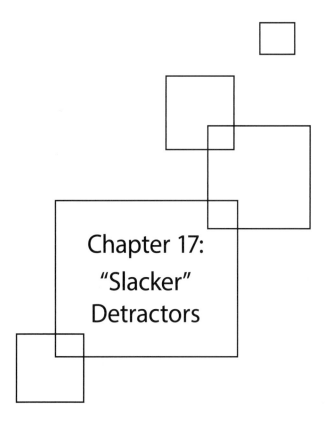

Chapter 17: "Slacker" Detractors

Dave has a great résumé with the right education and expertise from brand-name schools and employers. When he accepted your job offer, you felt like you made one of the best hires of your career.

Since Dave got the job, however, his talents haven't translated into the results you expected. The expertise you sensed in his interview is indeed present; he's a smart guy with great communications skills—at least his verbal communication skills. He's outspoken in team meetings and has many ideas, most of which seem to have potential. Interestingly enough, however, those ideas relate to other peoples' responsibilities. Dave's willingness to comment on how others are doing or not doing their jobs is drawing complaints from your team. He has much less to say about his own area. You've started seeing eyes roll every time Dave speaks. His teammates say he should spend more time tending to his work instead of thinking about theirs.

When it comes to written communications, Dave doesn't have much to say. Getting him to produce reports is frustrating. He's never met a deadline he didn't renegotiate. You schedule regular meetings with him to check on his progress with assignments. Those meetings turn into lively discussions about why the deadline is too tight, or they are debates on the merits of his assignments. If Dave put as much energy into his work as he did arguing with you about it, he would deliver phenomenal results.

Dave is content knowing how to do the job instead of actually doing it. He seems to think he's paid for being smart instead of for being productive. He has a strong reputation around your organization for being talented—you're surprised by how often he comes up in conversations with your colleagues. That's how you learned he networks extensively with other executives. It makes you wonder if he's looking for a new job. On his résumé, you noticed he switched jobs several times. You know Dave delivers outstanding performances in interviews. Maybe he'd rather rely on his interviewing skills to get new jobs because that's easier than *doing* a job. If he manages to get a raise every time he switches jobs, he may have found a lucrative alternative to working hard to advance his career. It may not be a sustainable approach, but it's worked for him so far. His failure to deliver is frustrating everyone.

You hate the thought of losing someone as talented as Dave, but his lack of results is alarming. His teammates have picked up his slack. You've dedicated more of your leadership capital than you'd like harping on him to get his work done. There's no doubt that Dave is a "Slacker."

Approaches for Leading a Slacker

Leading Slackers requires you to "**Unlock Motivation**" within them. Slackers have the capability to do their jobs well. If they applied themselves, Slackers could be Exemplars on your team. Turning Slackers around reduces the team conflict they create when they talk about everyone else's work instead of doing their own. Such a turnaround reflects well on your ability to develop people. If Slackers don't learn to deliver results, their careers will come to a grinding halt. Potential can only carry them so far. When they get their acts together, they can end up on a fast track to bigger roles. If you can build a reputation as someone who can get people out of slumps and advance their careers, you should attract positive attention—both from people who want to join your team and leaders who want you to join theirs.

To turn a Slacker around, first let him know his behavior isn't acceptable. If he's avoided deadlines in the past, give him a real deadline to hit or face the consequences. Prepare for that meeting the same way you would with other Detractors. Connect with your HR representative to start the performance improvement plan process. Document the expectations for the Slacker's role, his performance against those objectives, and the specific goals he needs to accomplish. Set deadlines for completing that plan and keeping his job. Make it clear that delivery of results is a condition of his employment. You're not looking to threaten him—you're merely explaining the cold, hard facts of his situation. Coach him that being smart isn't enough. Reassure him you believe he has the ability to do the job—if he sets his mind to it. Give him a picture of what success could look like for him.

The painful first conversation with a Slacker might be enough to turn her around. Or she might say she'll improve but she never does. That behavior requires you to escalate the situation and put her on a formal performance improvement plan. Contact your HR team for assistance with doing this. You'll need to follow your organization's process for documenting the Slacker's performance shortfalls and then provide her with the completed plan. After putting your Slacker on a formal performance improvement plan, have a frank discussion with her about how she wants to rectify the situation. Don't limit the discussion to her role on your team—discuss her career aspirations too. Let her know that if she plans to keep slacking by relying on her smarts and reputation to get her through, she's going to have a performance crisis that will be hard to recover from. If she doesn't change her behavior, it will kill her career at some point. If the combination of being put on a performance improvement plan and getting your frank assessment can't motivate her to behave differently, ask her what it will take to get her to change. If she's not interested in helping herself, you can't do it for her. These are potentially high-risk, high-return leadership investments.

Slackers have a decision to make that will determine your approach to leading them. If putting them on a performance improvement plan gets through to them, find the root cause of their problem. Maybe all that's holding them back is their motivation. They could be bored with their work. Maybe they lack the skills required to plan their work and manage their time. They might lack an important skill they convinced you they had but they actually don't. Perhaps someone else on the team is stealing credit for their work. Your discussion about root causes could give you insights on how committed they are to change. If they're defensive or in debate mode, they may be unwilling to do the hard work required. If they do commit to improving, take them at their word, but *don't* ease the expectations they've committed to meeting. If you sense a sincere desire to perform, make investments in their success. Get them a coach, send them to training, or find them a mentor. After all, they have the potential to become Exemplars. Investing your leadership capital and giving them the tools they need could deliver great returns.

If they're *not* going to work hard in their current role, help them find their next one. Work with them, in consultation with your HR team, to see what kind of referral you can give them. For external referrals, you can point to the Slackers' strengths. Leave it up to them to explain why they're leaving their role. For referrals for roles within your organization, give your candid assessment that this individual has the talent to be an Exemplar but he needs to turn around his performance to get there.

Case Example: Mikhail the Slacker

Mikhail was a smart guy—an extremely smart guy. He knew it, too. At the consulting firm where he worked, he had risen through the ranks faster than anyone thought possible. His ratings were consistently at the top end of the spectrum. Everyone wanted him on their project teams. Mikhail was known for working hard, putting in long hours, delivering creative solutions, and interacting well with clients. He was a Rising Star within the company.

When the exciting e-commerce strategy engagement for a major bank client was being staffed, Mikhail was a natural choice for a spot on the team. The engagement was fantastic at first. Mikhail was excited by the work and the team enjoyed working together. His workstream consisted of generating ideas for new service lines the bank could offer and building business cases to support those ideas. Mikhail went into the first progress review thinking he had ideas that would impress the client's leadership team. After the meeting, however, the client's team wasn't pleased. They didn't believe the first set of ideas—Mikhail's in particular—were innovative or compelling. They didn't understand why Mikhail was advocating so many "data services" ideas—they were a bank, after all. Mikhail was devastated by their opinions. To make matters worse, Mikhail's manager, Ankita, came down hard on him:

"Mikhail, you're supposedly one of the best consultants we have. I'm not seeing it. Your so-called 'insights' look like worn-out, rehashed ideas from the latest issue of

Fast Company magazine. I thought you were better than this. None of your analysis pages deserve to be in the main presentation. Heck, most of them aren't worthy of being included in the appendix. Fix it."

The following week, a different Mikhail showed up for work. He came in two hours later than usual and left at 6 p.m. when his normal departure time was around 9 p.m. He rehashed old presentations instead of trying to generate new ideas. He farmed out several of his deliverables to interns and didn't check the quality of the work they returned to him. Their spreadsheets came back riddled with errors. One intern submitted a spreadsheet in which all the cells were hard-coded instead of being formula-based. His "outsourcing" of his work was a disaster. Mikhail never caught the errors because he couldn't be troubled to check their work. "Why should I invest time in something the client won't read anyway?" he reasoned. When Ankita confronted him on his low output and poor quality, his response was a terse, "Well, if the client thinks my work isn't that great, what's wrong with giving them what they expect?" His poor performance continued unabated.

At the end of the engagement, Mikhail received the progress review rating he deserved. It wasn't pretty. Ankita did exactly what she should have by spelling out specific behavioral examples of his poor performance. The review included mentions of his failure to check his work, his poor attitude when receiving feedback, and his failure to meet quality standards. Every feedback point had a specific behavioral example to support it. She noted changes he needed to make to return to his high-performing ways. He would have to ensure he met quality standards, check his work, and interact with others in a more positive way. Cecily, Ankita's boss, knew it wasn't enough to tell Mikhail what needed to change. They needed to give him the opportunity and the support to do so. To their credit, they had Mikhail join them on their next project. He was thankful for the chance to prove himself. He found the next engagement's subject matter both challenging and intellectually stimulating. He was given clear performance expectations on the first day of the engagement. They included standards for timeliness, quality, and creativity. He knew what he had to do to succeed. Cecily and Ankita invested a great deal of leadership capital helping him turn out high-quality deliverables. His results improved dramatically as he began taking initiative again. He demonstrated he could still manage his own activities and generate great insights for the client. As his results improved, Cecily and Ankita reduced the amount of effort they were investing in him. By the end of the engagement, Mikhail was well on his way toward being a Rising Star again.

Ankita and Cecily led Mikhail through a difficult situation. They handled his Slacker behavior exactly as they should have. They gave him concrete examples of his unacceptable behavior, set clear expectations for his performance, and created opportunities for him to get back on track. Coaching him consumed time and energy, and they both invested additional leadership capital in his improvement. As his results improved, they reduced that investment accordingly. Mikhail's journey from Rising Star to Slacker then back to Rising Star is a great example of how it's a team member's *behavior* that lands them in a particular box rather than who they are as a person. Positions on the Leadership Matrix shift. Leaders have the ability to influence those shifts by changing how they interact with their team members.

How Slackers Impact Your Leadership Capital

Slackers consume excessive amounts of leadership capital because they don't deliver results. Their performance *requires* leaders to intervene. Leaders must follow up with Slackers to ensure they're turning out their deliverables. They have to coach and train Slackers. They must clarify, monitor, and explain their expectations and how Slackers are performing relative to them. Those conversations happen on a frequent basis because if they don't, the Slacker's behavior worsens. Without these leadership capital investments, Slackers create large risks for the team. Their work goes undone and others must pick up the slack, or customers don't get what they need. The team's morale can plummet as people become frustrated with Slackers' failures and their leader's inability to rectify the situation.

Don't avoid investing leadership capital in your Slackers. Do so as soon as you identify the problems they're causing. The faster you either turn their performance around or remove them from their role, the better. Your interactions with them will be tiresome. It's maddening to see someone who's talented squander her abilities and not even try to perform well. Get past your frustration and engage with them. Yes, that requires a big investment of your time, energy, and effort, but the return on that investment can be tremendous. You'll get your Slacker to generate results that move her out of that box to somewhere more productive on the Leadership Matrix. The rest of the team will appreciate your efforts. Making this required investment versus letting the situation continue will reduce the time you spend placating your team members while you reassign the Slacker's work onto their desks. Your entire team benefits when you make the right leadership capital investments to rectify a Slacker's poor performance.

By way of review, here's a reminder of the leadership approaches you should be applying for each behavior type you find on the Leadership Matrix. These approaches form the basis of your performance improvement plans and dictate how you'll invest your leadership capital going forward."

The Leadership Matrix

	Output: Team Member Results	
	High-Cost Producers "Squeaky Wheels": Wean "Steamrollers": Reduce Friction	**Exemplars** "Rising Stars": Promote Internally "Domain Masters": Nurture in Place
	Detractors "Square Pegs": Fill Skill Gaps "Slackers": Unlock Motivation	**Passengers** "Stowaways": Engage "Joyriders": Refocus

Output: Team Member Results — HIGH / LOW

HIGH   LOW

Input: Leadership Capital Invested

Part VII:
Applying the Leadership Matrix

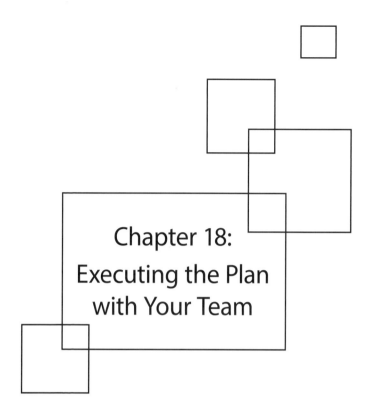

Chapter 18:
Executing the Plan
with Your Team

Once you have plotted your team members on the Leadership Matrix and have identified the approaches you'll use to improve their performance, put the plan into action. We recommend you follow a five-step process:

1. Document your assessments of where your team members fall on the Leadership Matrix.

2. Build a plan that defines the actions required for team members to improve their performance.

3. Discuss your approach with your team members and agree on the improvement plan.

4. Take the specified actions and execute the plan.

5. Measure and adjust as appropriate.

Those steps probably seem familiar if you've ever made a big decision or executed a project. Using the Lead Inside the Box method to improve your team's performance requires you to apply the same discipline you would if you were implementing a major initiative or making an important decision. Arguably, your efforts to improve your team's performance are as valuable as implementing a large technology or operational project. In both cases, you're improving your organization's capabilities in a way that will deliver ongoing value. That's an investment worth being rigorous about as you plan and execute that project.

One important point to remember as you implement your plan is that people should change positions on the matrix based on their performance. These shifts can happen quite rapidly. Having a well-thought-out plan for how you're going to invest your leadership capital and what behavioral changes you expect to see will aid you in accelerating these shifts.

Documenting Your Assessment of Team Member Positions

The first step in the process is conducting your assessment. Refer to the list of questions in Appendix A and assess each member of your team. As you answer the questions, look beyond recent events. Look back three to 12 months and think about their behaviors. When you answer a question, write down a few concrete examples of behaviors you've observed or are aware of to back up your assessment for that particular question. Be fact-based and rely upon actual events versus opinions or emotions as you answer the assessment questions. Documenting these behaviors will be time well spent. You'll use these examples later as you have your conversations with your team members about their behaviors and what they should change or continue doing.

Your perspective on your team member's performance is an important input into the assessment, but that's not all that should go into it. Look at their prior progress reviews and feedback documentation. Those reviews can be a valuable evaluative resource because they should contain behavioral observations that can serve as a basis for answering the assessment questions. Reviews you've written as well as those written by prior managers can be insightful. Prior managers may have seen behaviors of which you're unaware. Those additional perspectives will make your assessment more complete. Speak with the individual's colleagues—they see this person operate in situations you never will, and their observations will make your assessment more accurate.

The techniques for conducting this assessment are no different from the ones you would use during an annual appraisal process: Have team members answer the assessment questions about themselves. Their answers can serve as a useful point of comparison to the assessment you make. If there are major differences between your assessment and theirs, that's the first conversation you'll need to have. Ensure both of you are looking at their performance and evaluating it in the same manner. Probe more deeply into areas where your perspective and theirs are inconsistent. If they rate themselves better than you do, ask for examples to back up their assessment. Be open to changing your assessment—they might share achievements of which you weren't aware. Correspondingly, be prepared to share your observations and explain why those behaviors led you to the assessments you've made. This step isn't about who's right or wrong—it's about getting to a common understanding of their performance and reaching a fair assessment of their behaviors.

When you feel comfortable with your initial assessment of where the person belongs on the Leadership Matrix, plot his position. Don't worry about precise placement in the matrix, just focus on which of the four boxes his behaviors belong in and decide which behavioral subtype he demonstrates. For example, if he's a Passenger, is he more of a Joyrider or a Stowaway? To make that determination, consider his behaviors and observable examples that led you to that categorization. Be sure to capture that perspective in writing because it will influence how you lead this individual going forward. This initial assessment and documentation phase will help you after you've taken action. It should guide you during the "measure and adjust" phase as to which behaviors should have changed.

Building a Plan

You next need to build a plan to implement your desired changes. If you want meaningful change to happen, specificity is required. You're asking people to do something that is inherently difficult—change. Their behaviors have been shaped for extensive time periods. The way they act has become habit. In some cases, such as those of your Exemplars, those are great habits that you want to reinforce. In other instances, however, those habits need to be broken. Breaking those habits requires a clear articulation of what the new behaviors need to be, and those new behaviors need to be reinforced continuously. A clear action plan that defines the targeted behaviors and lays out situations in which the individual can demonstrate them increases their chances of successful change.

The first step of your plan is to document the highest-priority behaviors to focus on changing. Focus is critical. People can't work on improving too many behaviors at once; they'll end up doing many things poorly. This will then frustrate them. It could lead them to give up on the plan because they're not seeing progress on any of the 10 or 15 behaviors you're asking them to change. A good analog for the need to focus is training for a sport: A golfer doesn't work on every aspect of her game every practice. She focuses. She'll practice her long shots in one session and her short shots the next. Even within those disciplines she'll focus—she might focus on the movement of her lower body during practice rather than trying to improve her entire swing at once. Focus helps players improve results more quickly. Once they've mastered one element of their swing, they focus on improving the next. Your plan for your team member's improvement requires a similar level of focus. Note which behaviors need to change and what behaviors you would expect to see demonstrated once the situation changes.

In terms of selecting the prioritized behaviors to change, ask yourself the following questions after you've created the complete list of behaviors requiring improvement:

❑ Which of these behaviors is holding him back the most?

❑ Which behavior can he improve the most rapidly?

❑ Which one is most directly related to his core responsibilities?

❑ Which ones is he most interested in improving?

❑ Which one can you help him with the most?

Try to shorten the list to two or three focus areas. A list longer than that will be hard to make progress against. Team members can get overwhelmed if you ask them to work on too many improvements at once.

Once you have your focused list of desired changes, make those changes tangible by relating them to your team member's daily responsibilities. For each targeted behavior, think of specific projects or situations in which you'll ask your team member to make those changes. Remember—these changes are hard to make. One reason for that is your team member might not be sure which situations are good opportunities to try the new behaviors. They need your guidance. For example, if you tell her she needs to improve her public speaking skills because she tends to shy away from the spotlight, you'll need to guide her toward low-risk opportunities to build those skills. For her, every public speaking opportunity might seem terrifying. With your guidance, she might see that leading the conversation at one of your staff meetings is a safe place to try out these new skills. She'll also realize that leading the discussion about a controversial initiative at the senior executive steering committee meeting should wait until she's made progress in building her speaking skills. This preliminary list of situations will serve as the groundwork for your discussion with your team member on where you expect to see her changing her behaviors.

The burden of change doesn't solely rest on your team member's shoulders. You'll need to identify how *you* will behave differently in terms of how you're investing your leadership capital. Are your behaviors contributing to your team member's deficiencies? Is he failing because you're piling too much work on his desk? Are you an "enabler" who does the work for him rather than making him learn how to do it himself? You're responsible for aspects of the challenges he faces. If you understand how your behaviors drive his issues, you'll be able to change your actions while he focuses on changing his. The combination of both of you acting in a concerted effort to affect change has several positive effects: First, it can accelerate the improvements. Two people working on a problem at the same time can fix it faster than one person can. Second, there's accountability. If your team member sees you working hard to change your behavior, he'll feel an obligation to work as hard as you are to change his behaviors too. This dynamic works in both directions. If you see him putting in a great deal of effort to making his changes, your commitment to your own changes should feel that much stronger.

Discussing Your Approach

Your people shouldn't be recipients of the plan you create. You're not looking to dictate behaviors to them in a one-way communication. True change requires their commitment to the plan. This means they must understand the method you used to assess their performance and *they need to have input* into building the plan. They have to own the changes you're asking them to make. Sharing this method with your team members will put context around why you're suggesting the actions you're recommending. When you explain the approach, do so in the context of wanting to improve team performance. Tell them you want to help individual team members succeed and do a better job of investing your time and effort. When they understand how their actions fit into a broader context of helping everyone around them improve, the effort you're asking them to put in makes more sense. Such effort feels more important to them than if it was only about them changing for the sake of change.

Sit down with each team member individually and explain how the Leadership Matrix works. First, discuss the "output" axis of the Leadership Matrix. Your team members need to understand the results you expect them to deliver and how they are or aren't doing so. This conversation will feel as though you're delivering a performance review—that's because you are. Refer to goals they're accountable for achieving. Explain how you perceive their performance relative to those goals. Explain why you see them as exceeding, meeting, or falling short of achieving them. Precision matters. For example:

"Your goal was a 98% on-time rate for report delivery. In the past six months, you've achieved 98.7%. I know you've done so by making the reporting process more efficient through elimination of unnecessary reports and data queries. Those are great results."

Feedback such as that is constructive because your team member knows the *actions* she's taking to deliver the results. That knowledge gets her to focus on demonstrating the behaviors you expect from her.

Many times, the feedback will need to be corrective. The same precision principle applies:

"For the last three months you were responsible for leading Project Crystal. Those responsibilities include managing stakeholder expectations and incorporating their feedback into project deliverables. I've received feedback from seven of those stakeholders that you haven't had a single meeting with them about their input, nor have you reached out to them via email. Two IT managers and one Operations manager have also expressed concerns about how you manage meetings. They've said you shut down conversations with responses like, 'That's not important here. Can we please focus on the task at hand? You can deal with your issues after I get done defining the scope.' These comments haven't been isolated incidents. Your treatment of these team members has left them frustrated."

That feedback clarifies the expectation, the actions he took that fell short of it, and how his behaviors drove the situation's outcome. His placement on the Leadership Matrix should make sense to him based on those results. Additionally, he knows what he needs to change going forward to meet your expectations. This awareness will be an important component of the improvement plan you share with him in future aspects of this discussion phase.

Once your team members understand why you've placed them where you have on the "output" axis, explain the "input" axis that paints the picture of how you're spending your leadership capital. They need to appreciate how much time, energy, and effort you're investing in them. In our experience, many team members are surprised by this perspective. They often see your efforts as "something the boss is supposed to do." They may not recognize how their actions either save you time and effort or lead you to invest more in them if they're not doing well. Making them aware of your investments sets up the conversation you'll have later about how they should expect to see your behavior change. Concrete examples are a must during this discussion step. Saying, "You take up too much of my time" doesn't aid understanding. They won't be able to make real changes with ambiguous input like that. It's much more actionable for them if you instead say, "You take up more of my time than I think is appropriate. For example, in the past month you have scheduled twice-weekly hour-long update meetings with me on Project Excellence. That's a total of eight hours of updates. Many of those updates have consisted of a rundown of every project task, where your comment is, 'this is on track,' which is no different than the prior meeting. Those updates could be covered in an email or a much shorter meeting."

Armed with this new understanding of how *their* actions drive *your* behaviors and time investments, your team members will be more accepting of making changes that make more efficient use of your leadership capital. Explaining the Leadership Matrix method should put them at ease as to why you're asking for changes in their behaviors. They'll know your request is not for the sake of making your life easier but rather is for the greater good of the team.

Once you've explained the justification for their placement on both the "output" and "input" axes, you can show your team members where they are on the Leadership Matrix. When you do so, we suggest you *not* use the box or type descriptors. People might not react well if you tell them they're a Slacker, or they may get an overinflated sense of their own importance if you tell them they're a Domain Master. Instead, describe the axes of the Leadership Matrix and the behaviors that have led you to place your team members where you have. After you share why their behaviors place them in a specific box, explain how you'll work with them to improve their performance. Be as specific as possible about which behaviors need to change and how they should be behaving. For example:

"On Project Crystal, your behavior of shutting down conversations in meetings needs to change. Instead of telling people 'that can wait until I'm done with this,' try inviting their input. Maybe instead say, 'You raise a valid concern. Please tell me more about it so I can document it and ensure we account for those risks in future project stages.' As they share their perspective, write their thoughts down. Be sure to get back to them when you've formed a plan for addressing the concern. I know this new approach requires effort on your part. I'm going to help you make this change. I can observe your meetings to give you feedback on this behavior afterward if you're comfortable with me doing that. I'll solicit feedback from stakeholders every few weeks to see if you're making progress and how you can continue to improve. Let's use our weekly one-on-one time to discuss your performance. I can give you ideas on techniques for how to do this better."

That conversation can be powerful. You've identified situations in which this person can improve, provided examples of different behaviors that will meet your expectations, and offered to assist her with making changes so she knows she's not alone in taking on this task. After providing such feedback, be sure to ask her if she's willing to make these changes and if the support you're offering is sufficient. You need her commitment to the plan you're laying out.

The development plan is essentially a behavior contract between the two of you. It should specify behaviors, projects, expected results, and how you'll invest in this person to assist with the *highest priority changes* you're asking him to make. For simplicity's sake, create a chart with four columns. In the first column, list the top two to four behaviors he needs to change. In the second column, document specific projects, meetings, interactions, or deliverables where the two of you believe he can demonstrate these new behaviors. In the third column, write down the techniques he'll use or the new behaviors he'll demonstrate. In the fourth column, capture specifically how you will support him in his change efforts—for example, providing coaching, sending him to training, gathering and providing feedback for him, and so on. Both of you have obligations under this contract. This chart formalizes those obligations and makes it more likely those behaviors will remain in focus. The plan can now be a living document to which both of you refer during your progress review meetings. It's the plan's specificity that will drive the change you desire.

Taking Action and Executing the Plan

The hardest part of the whole process is executing the plan and monitoring performance relative to expected results. Both you and your team member are responsible for taking the actions you've listed on the behavior contract. Keep the contract handy. Refer to it often and ensure you're both taking advantage of opportunities to try out new behaviors. If you've asked her to lead meetings differently, check in before those meetings and remind her of the new behaviors. Be prepared to offer her techniques to try in the meeting. After the meeting, reconnect with her to see how the meeting went. Was she successful in applying the new behaviors? What did she find easy or difficult as she made her changes? Even if the meeting didn't go well, praise her commitment to making changes. Acknowledge it takes extra effort on her part to try to change the way she works. Let her know you don't take her efforts for granted. Behavior change can be a long and difficult road. Regular encouragement is part of your role in this process.

Give and receive regular feedback during the plan's execution. Athletes working on part of their game get instant feedback on whether the changes they're making are successful. A basketball player working to improve his foul shooting knows within a second if he made the basket or not. He can monitor his performance improvement by tracking the simple "percentage of shots made" statistic. Successful behavior change at work, however, is much tougher for your team members to assess. They need your assistance. Refer to the behavior contract and focus on the deliverables the two of you agreed upon as focus areas. Let her know if her new behavior met your expectations. If it did, praise her. If it didn't, explain how she came up short. Frequent feedback enables your team members to make adjustments more rapidly.

Measuring, Adjusting, and Taking Further Action

After a reasonable period of time, assess whether or not your team members are making progress toward the boxes they need to be in. For some behaviors, you'll review them sooner than others. For example, if they need to improve their ability to structure spreadsheets and formulas, you'll be able to assess improvement sooner than if you're looking for them to improve their public speaking skills. The former are fairly concrete skills that can be improved quickly. Public speaking skills, on the other hand, might take longer to build, and therefore your assessment period will be longer.

Evaluate your team members' individual behaviors relative to your initial assessments. Refer to your prioritized list of the top two to four behaviors you're asking them to change and assess each behavioral area on its own. Have they improved at all? Are they moving along the right trajectory? Are you investing a more appropriate amount of your leadership capital in them compared to the results you're seeing? Document your assessments. Write down specific observations you're using to make this updated assessment. You'll need to share these events with your team members as you explain your view of how their performance is or is not improving.

Monitor your team member's performance against the *entire* plan regularly. Take a step back and look at *all* the behaviors both of you are trying to change. Are you making satisfactory progress on all the behaviors—both yours and his—that the two of you agreed would change? Is it necessary to reprioritize your efforts or shift focus? Are your expectations still reasonable? Revisit your team member's goals periodically to ensure he's staying on track. If he's not, you'll need to take corrective measures. During this review you might find that he's made great progress on one of the behaviors and has failed to improve on another. In that situation you might refine the entire plan by removing the newly satisfactory behavior from it and agreeing to spend more time on the behavior that isn't improving as quickly. Prioritization is an ongoing effort. As behavior improvements on the list are completed, they come off the list and new behaviors are added. Remember—some new behaviors you might add to the list aren't necessarily current deficiencies but instead could be behaviors your team member needs to demonstrate to perform at the next higher level. Identify his next opportunities to build new skills so he can continue to grow.

Evaluate your own behaviors too. Part of this process involves you investing your leadership capital more efficiently. Look at the plan and your behaviors relative to the changes you committed to make. If you agreed to coach her on her Excel skills instead of fixing her spreadsheets on your own, have you followed through on that change? Document the areas you've improved upon and note any deficiencies you have as they relate to the execution of the plan.

We've always found it worthwhile to ask your team members to go through the same exercise of evaluating performance relative to the plan. Have them conduct the same assessment of their performance, your performance, and where they stand on progress against the plan. This self-assessment achieves several goals. First, it heightens their awareness of the targeted behaviors as they occur. That awareness in the moment enables them to behave differently than they would have in the past. Second, their self-assessment will provide you with better data for assessing their performance. They might highlight events of which you're not aware because you can't be around them 100-percent of the time. Third, their perspective on your behavior changes helps you change your behaviors more effectively. If you think you're being more hands-off and giving them coaching rather than doing their work, but they feel you're not coaching them enough, that will be an important conversation to have. You might still have improvements of your own to make. Your team members can highlight areas you might want to focus on.

Once both of you have conducted your assessments, sit down with your team member to discuss your findings. Discuss each behavior on the list. Note whether it has improved, stayed the same, or gotten worse. Share observable events to back up the assessment. If things aren't going well, work together to refine the plan. See if there are additional ways you can make him more successful. If behaviors have improved, take them off the list and agree upon the next behavior you'll both work on improving. Reprioritize your efforts. Write down and commit to the next set of changes you'll both make. Identify the opportunities to practice the new behaviors. Revise the behavior contract and repeat the process.

We encourage you to keep a dated copy of these reviews in your team members' files. You can refer back to these to look for patterns. In some cases you can use those trends to support your advocacy of promotions or increased responsibility for your team members. In other cases, you can use it as a documentation trail to take more formal corrective actions like putting them on performance improvement plans or removing them from their roles.

Here's an example of a common scenario: A team leader was trying to get a team member to perform at an acceptable skill level, but the team member exerted little effort to make the requested behavioral changes. This went on for several months. When the team leader went to his boss and Human Resources with a recommendation that the individual's employment be terminated, he was asked for documentation to support his assessment. He didn't have any. The result was he needed to spend several more months dealing with the team member's poor performance so he could establish a satisfactory documentation trail to support a termination. The team leader continued to invest time and energy into this Detractor but despite his best efforts, performance didn't improve. After three more months of poor performance, the team leader was able to get support for his termination recommendation —this time with appropriate documentation. If only he had been documenting performance from the beginning he wouldn't have had to deal with a prolonged poor performance period, stress, and a drain on his leadership capital. Documentation is key in such cases.

The Leadership Matrix points your team members in the right direction, but that doesn't always guarantee they'll get there. Sometimes leaders must manage team members out of the positions they're in if they can't get where they need to be. Leaders need to have people who can do the job filling those roles. Team members want to be in jobs in which they can succeed. Keeping someone in a role in which she's not successful isn't fair to anyone. The team member feels demoralized. The leader is harried. The team member's coworkers are upset that they have to pick up additional work or that they're not getting their fair share of the leader's attention. Leaders can't look at managing someone out of the organization in isolation, as if it relates only to that team member. It's difficult to fire someone, but failing to do so has broader implications. Leaders need to appreciate the impact of that person's performance on the *entire* team. The best choice for everyone involved could be to redeploy that team member to another part of the organization or even relieve her of her job. Sure, it's hard to do, but failure to make the difficult decision can harm everyone more than taking the required action of letting someone go.

Imagine you have a poor performer on your team—a true Slacker who is dragging everyone down. Instead of investing time improving him, firing him, or redeploying him to a more appropriate role, you decide to ignore him and hope the problem goes away. The rest of your team gets frustrated when they see you avoiding the issue. Why should they work hard and cover up the Slacker's mistakes? Rather than dealing with their increased workload and the perceived inequality of how you're treating the Slacker versus how you're treating them, your Exemplars decide to look for new jobs. Some of your High-Cost Producers become frustrated with the Slacker's lack of accountability. They adopt a mindset of "if he can get away with doing nothing, then maybe I shouldn't work so hard." Before you know it, their results plummet and you have a bunch of new Slackers on your hands. Your team's performance declines—all because you weren't willing to tackle the challenge of dealing with one team member who deserved to face serious consequences. Remember—none of your decisions happen in isolation. Every action you take impacts not only the team member you're focused on but also all the other team members too. Act accordingly.

Case Example of Executing the Plan

To illustrate how to perform the five steps of executing the plan, here's an example from Mike's experience.

I had a critical opening on my team that I needed to fill. Billy worked on a team in another division and he seemed to have the skills required for the role. Unfortunately Billy had been labeled as a low performer. During the last performance review cycle he was essentially designated as a Stowaway—he wasn't seen as turning out meaningful results. Billy had a reputation for doing the minimum required of him.

I knew Billy's manager wasn't spending much time with him. When I spoke to Billy about taking on the role, his eyes lit up and he seemed excited about the possibilities. He said, "This seems like a meaningful role. All I'm doing now is updating the same spreadsheets every month. Any time I want to make changes or take on new projects, my manager says no and tells me to focus on the reporting. To be candid, it's frustrating. I want a role where I can have an impact." After we discussed the role's responsibilities and my expectations of him, Billy accepted the position.

We built a performance improvement plan because both of us knew he had skill deficiencies. He also had to overcome negative perceptions others had of him. First, I documented why I believed he was behaving like a Stowaway. I wrote down the results I knew he had delivered in his prior role. It was a short list. I noted that it seemed as though he wasn't getting much leadership capital investment from his prior manager. The draft plan I created for Billy defined the behaviors both of us needed to change. For him, I noted his top two priorities were (1) demonstrating he could lead a major operational improvement project, and (2) showing he could manage large, disparate stakeholder groups. If he was able to demonstrate these two skills he would be delivering significant results, and others would see him doing so on a high-visibility project. To change his Stowaway behaviors, it was clear I needed to get Billy to engage. The behaviors I personally needed to demonstrate as part of this plan required me to invest more leadership capital in him. This would take the form of coaching him on how to engage stakeholders and how to break the big project into manageable chunks on which he could make progress every week. I was willing to commit a few hours per week to coaching him on these topics, although this was a significant investment of my time in one individual, considering I had many other team members I was responsible for leading.

Billy and I reviewed the plan and agreed upon the focus areas. He said the level of coaching investment I was willing to make was sufficient, but he asked for an additional leadership capital investment beyond that: "I'd appreciate it if you could advocate on my behalf and tell these five key stakeholders about my commitment to the project," he said. "I want them to know I'm engaged and excited to deliver great results. All five of them have a negative perception of me. I need your help overcoming that barrier." I agreed to deliver on his request.

As Billy worked on the project and I coached him and advocated for him, both of us got excited about his results. The project advanced quickly and Billy grew more confident in his abilities to lead the cross-functional team. He did a great job with managing his stakeholders. He attacked the project every day with a positive energy he hadn't demonstrated in a long time. I coached him regularly as we had agreed. Billy and I reviewed his progress every few weeks. To me it was clear he had engaged with his new role and had moved from being a Stowaway to more of a High-Cost Producer. I was investing a great deal of leadership capital in him. He was constantly in my office asking for guidance. Sure, those behaviors made him a Squeaky Wheel, but I was happy to see that behavior because now he was delivering results. As the project progressed, Billy needed less and less coaching from me. When we reviewed his progress after a few months I told him I was going to scale back the time I was investing in coaching him. From my perspective, I needed to wean him from the support I was providing. He agreed with my plan to step back and committed to continue to deliver results. I adjusted my behavior and dedicated less time to my coaching efforts, which reduced my leadership capital investment. After about six months, Billy completed the project. It wasn't without its difficult moments along the way, but compared to the complete lack of results he had demonstrated in his last role, his efforts were seen as outstanding. Eventually his delivery of results was consistent on multiple projects and he required little guidance from me. He was happy in his role and wanted to keep doing it. After a year of being on my team, I viewed him as a Domain Master. Going through the five steps of executing the plan with Billy took a great deal of effort on both our parts. It was worth the leadership capital investment.

Getting Billy to engage in the new role and step up the results he delivered, coaching him through his improvements, and then scaling back my support had a wonderful effect. He moved from Stowaway to Squeaky Wheel to Domain Master throughout the course of a year. By applying the approaches suggested in the Leadership Matrix, I got more out of Billy than either of us ever expected. Although it wasn't a straight path from Stowaway to Domain Master, both of us were flexible in our approach. We discussed his progress regularly and agreed upon the appropriate actions to take given where he was positioned on the Leadership Matrix. The results spoke for themselves.

The Leadership Matrix is a way to drive continuous improvement in your team and across an organization. It embeds evolution and ongoing personal development in your culture. Everyone on your team gets a view of their possible career paths. High performers have a goal for how to move on to their next challenge or to be more efficient in their current role. Low performers are given a mandate to move up to meet expectations or to move out so you can get someone in the role who can deliver results. Hopefully those poor performers can find roles for which they're better suited if they're not up to the challenge of improving their performance as a member of your team.

Great sports franchises that have stood the test of time do so by reinventing themselves through player changes every year. Those top teams are developing their potential talent, keeping their top talent satisfied, and moving out players who aren't meeting expectations but may be able to blossom with another team. The Leadership Matrix gives you the roadmap for how you can turn your own team into a champion in your organization. If you're rigorous in assessing your team members' performance, shifting where you're spending your leadership capital and how you're spending it, and executing performance improvement plans, your team's performance should improve. They'll deliver better results and you'll have more time and energy to dedicate to other pursuits such as stepping into roles of greater responsibility or achieving a better work-life balance.

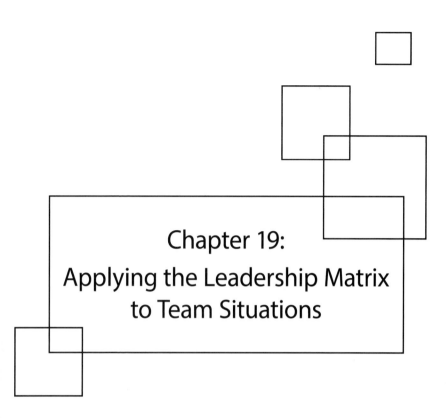

Chapter 19:
Applying the Leadership Matrix to Team Situations

Throughout the course of your career, you'll find yourself in many different team situations. Some of them will be of your choosing. Others will be thrust upon you. When new team situations arise, they can be overwhelming. The faster you're able to assess your team and prioritize your leadership efforts, the more rapidly you'll achieve team stability and drive results. The Leadership Matrix can be a powerful tool for focusing your leadership capital investments.

Let's explore the more common team situations you might find yourself in and how you can apply the Leadership Matrix to lead more efficiently and effectively.

Situation 1:
An experienced leader taking on responsibility for a new or existing team

When assuming responsibility for an existing team or building a new one, leaders can use the Leadership Matrix to assess what their talent portfolio looks like. Go through the assessment process for all of your team members. If you lead a multi-level team in which your direct reports have teams of their own, perform the assessment for multiple levels. You need an understanding not only of where your direct reports are on the Leadership Matrix, but also where *their* team members are. You may encounter situations in which your direct reports have teams containing disproportionate numbers of Exemplars, Passengers, Detractors, or High-Cost Producers. This can prove to be quite informative. For example, if you have one direct report whom you assess as a Slacker and find many of his team members are Passengers, there's likely a correlation there—your direct report is having trouble leading his team, and his team members might be taking advantage of that leader by coasting. That's the kind of situation in which you might replace that leader with someone who will do a better job of holding the team accountable for delivering results. Or you can coach your direct report on how to hold his people more accountable and change the behaviors of those Passengers so they're more productive. Usually the leader's performance and capabilities have a direct effect on the behaviors of his teams. If you can understand both levels of the team and how they're behaving, you can take more effective actions to improve that entire team's performance.

Based on your assessment of multiple levels of your team, you can determine how you'll spend your time to improve the team's performance. If you have a Rising Star leading a team full of Domain Experts and other Rising Stars, leading that team requires little time and energy. Instead focus your efforts on teaching that previously mentioned Slacker how to hold his team members accountable. High-priority steps such as managing out low performers or setting clear expectations and holding people accountable to meeting them can yield rapid results. In that situation, those kinds of skills are ones your Slacker might find useful as he tries to change his team's dynamics. That kind of differential leadership capital investment is an effective application of the insights you glean from the Leadership Matrix.

After stabilizing the team and improving poor performance, you can be deliberate with your investments in higher performers. Find opportunities to include them in the talent-development agenda. For example, activities like setting up mentoring and coaching relationships within the team with the goal of improving individual performance and team dynamics can pay huge dividends. Look for opportunities to have your Exemplars lead lower-performing team members. It's a great development opportunity for your Exemplars and it improves the team's performance with little investment of your personal leadership capital.

By way of example of how to use the Leadership Matrix when taking over a new team, let's look at the real experience of Kristene. She's a senior executive with a successful track record of leading people and delivering results. She left her job to take over a new team at a larger company. In her first few weeks, Kristene reviewed two years' worth of progress reviews written about her team members. She had one-on-one conversations with each of her new direct reports and conducted skip-level interviews with their team members. Her assessment proved enlightening. She had one team member, Frank, who was a Detractor. He demonstrated Slacker attributes but also exhibited Square Peg behaviors. Kristene wasn't sure which one he truly was. Frank's team members were frustrated by his "incompetence" and his "that's the way we've always done it" mindset. Frank believed he was an outstanding performer because he had indeed done a great job—in his last role. He could rattle off all the leadership tasks he should have been performing, but he didn't seem to have the ability to get any of them done.

Kristene had two other team members, Cindy and Marisol, who were filling interim roles. Both had been promoted provisionally to positions of increased responsibility but they weren't given the title, authority, or compensation to go along with their expanded roles. Consequently their team members didn't give them the respect they were due. Cindy's and Marisol's positions were viewed by everyone as temporary probation periods for management to evaluate their performance. Kristene saw that both Cindy and Marisol could be Rising Stars under the right conditions, but their "interim" titles were holding them back.

After a week of thoughtful planning, Kristene set out to improve her team's performance. First, she removed the obstacles Cindy and Marisol faced. Kristene lobbied senior management to make their roles permanent. She made a strong case for doing so by providing her leaders with evidence of great results they had delivered in the six months prior to Kristene's arrival. Senior management approved the promotions and removed the "interim" designation from their roles. Once promoted, Cindy's and Marisol's team members began giving them the respect they deserved. Their teams took instructions much more easily, and Cindy and Marisol were able to lead more effectively. Kristene's small leadership capital investment to promote her Rising Stars internally paid great dividends. Once she saw Cindy and Marisol take charge, she got out of their way to let them deliver the outstanding results she knew they were capable of delivering. Kristene then turned her attention to Frank.

Frank received a strong message from Kristene—start delivering results or risk losing your role. She documented her performance expectations and asked Frank what he would need in the form of her support to achieve those performance levels. He asked, "Can you give me space to let me run my team? I feel like I'm under a microscope. It's ruining my credibility with my people. I'm spending too much time updating management on my activities and not enough time running my operations." Kristene told him she would help him in a manner he found most effective. After a month of giving Frank "space," Kristene saw no noticeable improvement in his performance. If anything, he had gotten worse. With less direct supervision, Frank spent more time out of the office. His team members often didn't know where he was. Fortunately, Kristene documented Frank's lapses, gave him explicit expectations in writing, and had him sign off on every performance improvement feedback session. After one more month it was clear Frank had no interest in moving out of his Slacker role. He left Kristene with no alternative other than terminating his employment—which she did. Frank's team was elated with the decision. After Frank's departure, Kristene divided his responsibilities between Cindy and Marisol. Both their teams flourished.

It was Kristene's assessment of her team, her prioritization of key performance issues, and her disciplined execution of the improvement plan that enabled her to make rapid positive changes in her team's performance. Her actions earned her a great deal of respect around the company. People commented, "We're glad you took control of the situation and did what had needed to be done for a long time. You're the first leader to take over that team who identified the real issues and did something about them."

Situation 2:
A new leader recently promoted to take over her existing team and manage former peers

Making the leap from peer to boss can be awkward. People who were your buddies the day before now report to you. Leaders who find themselves in this situation can use the Leadership Matrix to remove emotion from the situation. They can assess their former peers and their peers' teams more objectively and determine where they need to spend their time and energy.

When changing role from peer to boss, there are many challenges. You will have difficulty separating your friendship from your leadership role. You might find yourself wanting to continue "hanging out" with your former peers. Some leaders overcompensate for the role change by staying "buddy-buddy" with the people they now lead. Doing so erodes credibility and authority. Maybe you hang out with them because it's comfortable. The risk in doing so is that time is a large portion of your leadership capital. If you're spending all your time hanging out with your former friends who are high performers, such activities come at the expense of investing your time in people who might need more of it for coaching and skill building. Another challenge of going from peer to boss is that making difficult decisions becomes even harder. While it's hard to discipline a team member, it's even harder to take disciplinary action against friends. They'll often appeal to your friendship and ask, "Can't you cut me some slack, pal? I mean, we're still friends, right?" That's an aw-fully sticky situation. The last common dynamic in this situation is passive-aggressive jealousy. Face it—you got the promotion and they didn't. They might resent you for it. They may even want you to fail so they can have a shot at the position. You could face Slacker, Steamroller, or Stowaway behaviors demonstrated by your former peers.

We encourage leaders who move from peer to boss to conduct a Leadership Matrix assessment on their teams—for both first- and second-level reports. Get an objective sense for the results your team members are delivering. Think through how you're going to invest your limited leadership capital. These situations call for you to be judicious in where you spend your time and energy. Remember—this is a larger role for you. Much of your time and effort will be spent learning your new job. You may have been a Rising Star before the promo-tion, but you might find you're a Square Peg or a High-Cost Producer as soon as you get your new title. Adapting to your new role leaves less time and energy for you to spend on your team members. Invest that limited lead-ership capital wisely! Once you have a sense for where your team members are on the Leadership Matrix, agree on a plan for how you'll spend your time and energy. Set their expectations and follow through on holding them accountable for the results you expect them to deliver.

One leader we're familiar with—we'll call her Leigh—made the jump from peer to boss. She was great friends with her three coworkers, Harry, Brent, and Marcy. Everyone on the team knew Leigh was a Rising Star and expected her to be moved into the next open Director's role. Soon a reorganization announcement was made and it included Leigh's promotion notice. The new organization chart had Harry, Brent, and Marcy reporting to Leigh, and all three of them had new roles. It was a lot of change to swallow all at once.

Leigh sat down with her new team and acknowledged the situation's awkwardness. She told them she'd be open and fair yet would expect their full support and continued great performance from them. Everyone wrapped their heads around the change and got excited about the work ahead. Leigh's first self-assigned task was assessing the results her people were capable of and how much of her leadership capital she would need to invest in them. Her initial assessment told her Harry was a Rising Star, Brent was a Square Peg, and Marcy was a Squeaky Wheel. Harry had run operations similar to the ones he was newly responsible for. She expected him to continue delivering great results and he wouldn't need much input or guidance from her. Brent's role was new territory for him. He came from a technology background but he'd been put in charge of an operational function with a large team of front-line personnel. He was clearly uncomfortable with the new role. Leigh knew she would have to invest time coaching him on how to be effective. Marcy was familiar with the type of work her new role required but she had a habit of asking permission before making decisions. She gathered excessive amounts of input and guidance from her prior boss on even the smallest of initiatives. Leigh didn't see the behavior changing easily. She knew she would see Marcy in her office quite often.

Marcy had always delivered results in the past, but they came with high interaction costs.

During the first few months in her Director role, Leigh gave Harry space. He was happy to have Leigh's trust and the freedom to lead his team how he saw fit. The results he delivered on his first few projects were outstanding. Leigh met with Brent several times a week to discuss how to lead a front-line operations team. She taught him her most effective techniques for inspiring front-line personnel. As he applied these new approaches, Brent became more comfortable in the role. Leigh was able to scale back the amount of time she invested in coaching him. As far as Marcy, Leigh told her, "I trust your capabilities, Marcy. What I'd like you to start doing more of is making decisions on your own and then updating me once you've made them." Leigh told her the reason for this was she wanted Marcy to build her leadership and decision-making skills. The only way for Marcy to do so was to make decisions on her own. Each week, Leigh noticed fewer and fewer interruptions by Marcy. Eventually, Marcy was making many more decisions without assistance. She still came to Leigh for guidance, but it was much less frequent than it had been during the first few weeks after the reorganization. Leigh's use of the Leadership Matrix and the suggested leadership techniques steered her through a tricky situation. She maintained her positive working relationships with her co-workers while getting great performance out of them at the same time.

This use of the Leadership Matrix shows leaders in a peer-to-boss situation how to avoid the pitfalls of not making difficult choices because someone was a friend the day before. Leigh could have avoided having those tough conversations with Marcy or sidestepped the issue of needing to coach Brent because he lacked skills. Instead, the Leadership Matrix highlighted these behaviors that needed to be changed and enabled Leigh to build a fair plan for making these improvements. You can be as effective as Leigh by taking a similar approach.

Using the Leadership Matrix can diminish a leader's potential bias to spend all his time with his high-performing friends when he should instead be spending his time improving lower performers. It would have been easy for Leigh to spend all her time working with Harry; he did a great job, exuded positive energy, and required little effort from Leigh. It would have been a huge mistake for Leigh to spend her time that way. The Leadership Matrix kept her from making that mistake by pointing her toward investing her limited leadership capital where it was most needed—working with Brent and Marcy to improve their skills. Should you face a similar peer-to-boss situation, look to the Leadership Matrix for guidance on where to spend your time and energy.

Situation 3:
A reorganization of people or work

Quite often, departments are combined or split, or a team's purpose is redefined. Reorganizations are disquieting. A change of routine or structure distracts people; it causes them to focus more on the organizational changes than on their responsibilities. Leaders in this role face several challenges the Leadership Matrix can help them overcome: First, they have to evaluate the performance of team members with whom they haven't worked before. Second, as responsibilities change, a team member who was a high performer on one set of tasks might find herself struggling with her new role. The Leadership Matrix makes it easier for leaders to assess these new team dynamics and apply their energy appropriately.

When a reorganization occurs, people jockey for position. Some do so by making their case for a new set of responsibilities they're well-suited for and that advance the organization's goals. Other people will position themselves with more selfish intent. They'll try to get bigger titles, more pay, less work, a nicer office, or other perks that benefit only them and do nothing to improve the organization. Many times this behavior comes in the form of them promoting their own capabilities and talking down about the abilities of people they view as obstacles to achieving their personal agenda. The reason they get away with this behavior is because many reorganizations result in someone new leading the team. That leader can be overwhelmed with his new organizational responsibilities. He doesn't have time to make fully informed decisions on how to allocate work. The easiest way to split up tasks is to let people make their case for what they should be responsible for—but doing so can be a huge mistake. Imagine a smooth-talking Slacker making a compelling case for reducing her workload because she's "unfairly had too much put on her plate." Or consider a Joyrider hijacking the team's agenda by advocating for a bunch of "exciting" projects that are "more important" than the other boring initiatives on the priority list. There could be an introverted Domain Master who isn't comfortable staking his claim and finds his work parceled out to less qualified people. Bad things can happen during a reorganization! If a leader doesn't assess her talent and instead relies upon people making a case for how their roles are defined, that leader can make the problem worse. You can use the Leadership Matrix to assess your new team members, especially if you haven't worked with them before. One of your primary goals when you lead a team through a reorganization is defining roles quickly and in a manner that puts everyone's talents to best use. The Leadership Matrix can be a powerful tool for making that happen.

During your assessment of the new team, watch out for negative impacts arising from changing someone's role. As you shift around responsibilities, be aware of situations in which you might be giving someone more than he can handle. If you have a Rising Star who's great at financial analysis and your reorganization calls for him to take on a front-line operating role, you might now have a Square Peg or a Squeaky Wheel on your hands. That former Rising Star must now master his new responsibilities, and he may have a tough time grasping his new role's intricacies and will need support from you to make the transition. If he makes the shift successfully, he's still a Squeaky Wheel—delivering results but only with substantial assistance from you. If he doesn't catch on, you've got a Square Peg to deal with. He'll have trouble delivering results despite the large amounts of leadership capital you invest in him. We're not saying you shouldn't change your new team members' roles. Such changes can be great growth opportunities. What we are advocating is being aware of the possible shift in a person's performance that is a result of his new responsibilities. If you know this risk exists, you can take mitigating actions before it becomes a major problem.

Sally serves as a great example of what can happen if a leader isn't mindful of a reorganization's impact on a team's performance. She was responsible for running the operations group in a business unit at a professional services firm. During a major reorganization, Sally's boss, the business unit president, was moved to another role in the company. Sally then took over his role as the business unit president. Her team now consisted of the operations group she previously led, a strategy group, an infrastructure group, a finance group, and a marketing group.

Before the reorganization, Rose led both the strategy and infrastructure groups. During the year prior to the reorganization, Rose demonstrated she was a Rising Star. At the beginning of that year, her responsibility was running the strategy group. As the year progressed, Rose took on greater responsibilities every month. Eventually she ran both the strategy and infrastructure groups. Her results were fantastic. Every week she found new ways to deliver more value to the organization.

When Sally took over the business unit, she wanted to show everyone she was in charge. She felt a bit insecure in her new role and felt the best way to demonstrate competence was to exercise her newfound authority. For her, this meant unilaterally changing Rose's role. Sally didn't solicit any input from Rose even though she had previously been a peer. Instead, Sally decided on her own to break Rose's team up and reassign responsibilities for the infrastructure group. Instead of reporting to Rose, that team would now report directly to Sally. Rose's role was reduced back to what she had a year ago—she was now only responsible for the strategy group. Rose found this demoralizing. She asked Sally to reconsider the reorganization and voiced her frustration with the move. Sally's response was, "Well, I'm running the team now. I think it makes more sense this way. You go focus on strategy and leave the infrastructure to me." Sally wasn't going to budge on her decision.

Rose gave up any hope of succeeding in the environment Sally had created. Her career path had been derailed and there was nothing she could do about it. She went from being a Rising Star to being a Slacker. She stopped putting forth her usual tremendous efforts and instead began looking for a new job. Sally pushed Rose to focus on the strategy group but Rose's heart wasn't in it. After a couple of months, Rose left the company to go pursue her own entrepreneurial venture, where her growth wouldn't be limited the way it was with Sally. By failing to assess the impact reorganizing the team would have on her high performers, Sally lost a great talent. That loss led others to leave the organization too. Sally's team's performance dropped precipitously as high performers fled to roles where they felt more supported by their leader.

Sally's failure to evaluate her team members' performance and how she should interact with them had disastrous results. After a year of running the business unit, Sally was removed from the role by senior leadership. Had she conducted a thoughtful assessment of the situation before acting, she might have realized how her changes could affect her Rising Stars, which could have prevented the exodus of talent from the team. If you're leading a reorganization, be sure to avoid Sally's mistake. Spend time assessing your new team using the Leadership Matrix and weigh the effects of changing responsibilities before you take action.

Situation 4:
A leader facing a crisis such as a need for layoffs

Layoffs, downsizing, and redundancies—whatever they're called, they suck. There are few professional tasks harder than telling someone he's losing his job. Navigating these situations requires a delicate touch to make decisions fairly and in a manner that's best for the organization. During a major crisis, a leader can use the Leadership Matrix to determine which people should be retained and which ones should be redeployed, including out of the organization. Although these are weighty decisions that no one likes to make, as leaders we're often put in the position of having to make these choices. By using the Leadership Matrix as part of the decision-making process, leaders reduce the possibility of making decisions based on emotion. They can instead rely on a more logical approach designed to improve the average performance of the team and free up leadership capital in the process. This occurs when low performers are removed and work is reallocated in a manner that motivates high performers.

If you find yourself in the unenviable position of having to lay people off, reduce their hours, convert people from full-time to part-time, or any other personnel-reduction action, take the time to assess your team using the Leadership Matrix. Use Appendix A of this book or the assessment at *www.leadinsidethebox.com/assessment* to conduct the full assessment of every person on your team who could be affected by the layoff. Document where each person falls on the Leadership Matrix. Identify if the person is a Rising Star, Domain Master, Slacker, Steamroller, and so on. Once you've done so, create a visual representation of the output—draw your team members' positions on the Leadership Matrix on a private white board or on a piece of paper. This output is your personnel inventory.

Now that you have a clear sense of your personnel inventory, draw your future organization chart on the same white board or another piece of paper. If you need to have an organization with 10-percent fewer people, draw it accordingly. Draw one box for each role on the future team. When you draw this new structure, focus on what the best structure is to achieve your future goals. Try not to think of which team member is currently occupying a position on the organization chart. Design the organization to meet your future operational and strategic needs. For each box, make notes about the skills required to perform that role. Again, try to forget about who's presently occupying the role. Instead think about the profile of the ideal person for that position. Once you have a picture of that future state complete, it's time to start filling boxes with names. Start with your Exemplars. Place your Domain Masters in roles you know they'll be capable of doing and excited about taking on. Next, look at your Rising Stars. Are there opportunities to give them bigger roles to advance their careers? Does a vacancy create an exciting new spot for them to fill? If you can take a risk on a Rising Star and give her more responsibility, a new organization structure after a layoff is a good chance to do so. Be careful you don't stretch those Rising Stars too far—you could turn a Rising Star into a Square Peg because she doesn't have the capabilities required to perform in the expanded role.

After you've placed your Exemplars, look next to your High-Cost Producers. Even though they frustrate you and consume much of your leadership capital, they still deliver results. These team members will usually fall into logical roles, but don't miss an opportunity to change someone's role if doing so will reduce the amount of leadership capital he requires. Perhaps have one of your Squeaky Wheels report to a Rising Star who's been placed in a bigger role. Maybe you can assign a Steamroller to a team where you know she'll create less conflict. If reasonable moves similar to that can be made, pursue them as appropriate. Unless you're making a huge reduction in force, all your Exemplars and High-Cost Producers should have roles.

For your next set of assignments, figure out where you're going to place your Square Pegs, your Joyriders, and your Slackers. Your Square Pegs aren't delivering results because they don't have the skills required for their current role. See if there are ways to move them to roles on the new organization chart that are better suited to their abilities. That kind of move can improve the results they're delivering and should result in you having to invest less leadership capital in them than you presently are. For your Joyriders, look for roles that may be a better fit with their interests or roles that are more clearly structured to prevent them from pursuing "shiny object" types of projects. For example, if you have a Joyrider in a role where he's supposed to focus on generating reports but he's off chasing projects involving the organization's social media efforts, maybe during the reorganization you can move him to the corporate social media team, as that's a better fit with where his passions lie. A more structured role can focus a Joyrider on delivering the results you expect. For your Slackers, hopefully you have an understanding of what motivates them. If they're in a team leadership role but they would much prefer to be an individual contributor, consider giving them a role where they can do so. Clearly they're talented—but they're not motivated to demonstrate those talents. We're not saying to reward bad behavior, but if there's an opening that can address a Slacker's unmet motivational needs, that move might be exactly the right choice to make to get her delivering results.

At this point in your process of filling boxes, the pickings are getting slim. Most team members without a spot at this point are your Stowaways or your Slackers. This is how the process should work. If people aren't delivering results, remove them from their roles or change their roles. Focus your leadership capital investments in team members who are meeting your expectations. Before you go moving Stowaways and Slackers into the remaining empty boxes on your new organization chart, ask yourself if doing so is the wisest decision. Would you be better off removing that Stowaway or Slacker from his role and seeking out a Rising Star being redeployed from another team? Can you leave the role vacant and recruit a better performer from outside the organization? Don't keep low performers around because you have a box to fill on the org chart. Look at the layoff as an opportunity to upgrade the talent of your entire team. Yes, these decisions are hard to make. You can either take the easy way out by laying off people indiscriminately, or you can be thoughtful, rigorous, logical, and deliberate about the changes you make. The latter approach is a more effective way to manage your talent portfolio. You can get the best out of your resulting team while reducing the amount of leadership capital you spend to get those results. Using the Leadership Matrix to conduct this assessment should help you achieve that desirable outcome.

The Benefits of Using the Leadership Matrix to Manage Your Talent

The Leadership Matrix and its associated assessment method can help you make good people decisions, especially in challenging situations. It can give you a clear picture of what your talent portfolio looks like as well as provide you with an understanding of where you're investing your leadership capital. Armed with those insights, you'll be able to make better decisions about the best roles for your team members. Shift where you invest your leadership capital to get better results from your team members.

As you apply the Leadership Matrix method, it truly can be a talent portfolio management tool. In financial investing, having a balanced portfolio of stocks, bonds, and funds with appropriate asset allocation is a core tenet of a successful investment strategy. The same principles apply to talent management. It's important to strive for balance across the boxes of the Leadership Matrix in your team. If you're fortunate enough to have more people in the top boxes, you may have room to bring in a new Slacker to grow into a higher performer. It's counterintuitive to add low performers to your team, but that's the essence of leadership—taking on the responsibility of getting people to achieve their potential while at the same time improving the organization's capabilities. You're not only helping others and improving the company with this approach, but you're also demonstrating your skill and courage, which differentiates you from other leaders and puts *you* in the Exemplar box. It's a virtuous circle: You help others improve. By doing so, you improve your leadership skills. Because of that, more people seek to join your team. Your team will be seen as a talent pool for the rest of the organization. Your responsibilities and influence grow as a result, and you're given opportunities to lead more people. In the process, you advance your career and the careers of your team members while at the same time improving the company's performance. We're not saying doing all that is easy, but we *are* saying it's worthwhile.

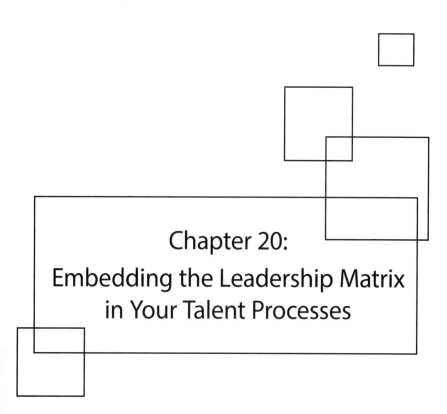

Chapter 20:
Embedding the Leadership Matrix in Your Talent Processes

Great leaders think about talent management every day. Certain processes and activities are collectively designed to build your team members' capabilities, and the Leadership Matrix can be used to support these talent-management and professional-development processes. Note we're *not* saying the Leadership Matrix is a *replacement* for any of your human-resource or talent-management processes—it's a tool you can use to get more out of those existing processes. If you use it to complement your current talent-management activities, you can get better answers about how to develop people, how to organize your teams, whom to hire or not hire, and how to coach your people so they can have successful careers.

There are four common talent-management processes that lend themselves well to incorporating Leadership Matrix assessments as additional inputs:

1. Hiring
2. Development planning
3. Succession planning
4. Career pathing

Hiring

The characteristics described in the Leadership Matrix are useful behaviors to look for in candidates you're considering. Ask questions that can give you insights into where you think a candidate might belong in the Leadership Matrix if he joined your team. Look for perspectives on his skills, will, relationships with peers and managers, ability to focus, and level of engagement with his work. When you discuss his previous roles and managers with him, try to get an understanding of how his past managers worked with him and which styles worked best. If a candidate describes several leaders who were "constantly accessible" and says, "I was in their office all the time talking about the projects I was working on. It was great having that level of access," you might be sitting across from a Squeaky Wheel. If his reason for leaving his last role was he "wasn't being challenged enough because the talents I have weren't appreciated," you could have a Slacker on your hands. Based upon their responses, ask yourself how his interactions with his leaders could lead him to perform for you.

Evaluate how the candidate's skills and prior results fit with your open position. Failure to do so can even make hiring a Rising Star a huge mistake. How? Imagine you're interviewing a Rising Star and you can't wait to make the job offer. As you reflect upon the role you're offering her, you realize it's limited in scope and advancement opportunities. The position is for an existing process that needs to be maintained. Additionally, you have several other Rising Stars already on your team. They're pursuing all the new opportunity areas and initiatives you've identified as priorities for the next 12 months. If this new Rising Star joins your team to fill your open process-management role, it could be a catastrophe. The role will be exciting for a few months until she figures it out. Once that challenge has been overcome and she begins looking for her next growth opportunity, you won't have much to offer her. Even worse, you might tell her to "stay focused on your core responsibilities because you're doing a great job with them." You've just turned that Rising Star into a Slacker. The lack of a growth trajectory destroys her motivation and within a few months she's off interviewing for a role on another team. Being mindful about the Leadership Matrix during your interviews can prevent you from making mistakes like this.

The Leadership Matrix can also help you sell opportunities to people because you can explain why it's a perfect role for them. You might say to a person who was a Slacker in his last job, "It sounds like your prior role was frustrating because you weren't able to work on projects related to emerging technologies. It seems like that kind of work is motivating for you. That's exactly the kind of work you'll be able to do in this role." That Slacker should find your role quite attractive—so much so that he's more of a Rising Star from day one on your team.

Development Planning

Applying the Leadership Matrix can help you produce a clear set of development objectives for each of your team members. It can help you highlight the skill and behavioral gaps they need to focus on. From that assessment, you can identify a targeted set of training, mentoring, or other development tools to offer. This process is about making your team better. The faster you can define where your team members' gaps are and select an effective approach to filling them, the more rapidly they'll improve.

Consider a situation in which you're trying to get a Steamroller to work more effectively with her teammates on a project team. When you realize the reason you're investing a great deal of leadership capital with her is that you're spending several hours every week fielding complaints from your Steamroller's teammates, the costs of her skill gap are clear. As you listen to the feedback you're getting, you recognize your Steamroller is offending people because of cultural insensitivity—she's from Eastern Europe and most of her teammates are from Latin America. She thinks she's being efficient by assigning tasks, checking on progress with short emails or text messages, and addressing people by the group they represent rather than using their first name. Her team-mates find his approach rude, brusque, impersonal, and domineering. They agree she's doing a great job getting results, but everyone is complaining that she's making life miserable in the process.

When you understand the root of the issue, you can design a developmental intervention to fix the problem. You might send your Steamroller to a class on appreciating different cultures in a business environment. You could provide her with a book on the subject. Maybe one of her teammates would be willing to coach her on how to better interact with her Latin American colleagues. After the targeted developmental intervention, you'll have a team member who delivers results and needs less of your leadership capital to do so. Once you've solved the near-term issue, you can work with your Steamroller to plan future developmental situations to make her a better performer. Good opportunities could be a rotational assignment to Latin America, transferring to work for a manager from Asia, or being mentored by one of your peers who faced similar challenges of his own in the past. The Leadership Matrix identifies the performance gaps so you can recognize how you want your team member's performance to change. That knowledge informs the developmental plan you create with her.

Succession Planning

Think about the last time there was a position vacancy in your organization. Was there an immediate short list of possible successors? Was the role filled quickly, or did it require an extensive search? People don't think about succession planning until it's too late. The purpose of any good succession planning process is twofold: First, it's to minimize the amount of time a role stays vacant and work goes undone while the organization scours the talent market for a replacement. Second, succession planning highlights positions that could become vacant due to performance issues and generates a plan to mitigate the risk of a departure. The Leadership Matrix can help you achieve both of these objectives.

When evaluating key positions and identifying successors, turn to your Leadership Matrix assessment for guidance. The group of Rising Stars one level below the possible vacancy is a natural pool to look for replacements if that individual leaves her role. You can also consider Rising Stars in other departments—those individuals might jump at the chance to change departments and learn a new functional area. Beyond the Rising Stars, be open to hiring Square Pegs who are in roles at a similar level. For example, if you have an Operations Manager who is viewed as key talent and he departs his role, his Finance Manager peer can be a replacement even though she's a Square Peg in the finance role. Why? She came from an operations background before she took the finance job and she's been foundering in that role since she took it. A move back to operations might be exactly what she needs to turn her performance around. Team members' positions on the Leadership Matrix can be good indicators of who should or shouldn't be on your short list of replacements for key roles. If you want to further develop the high performers on your team, get other leaders to include your Rising Stars in their succession planning talent pool. That list is a useful resource for other leaders when they're looking to fill gaps in their teams. This gives your high performers the visibility they deserve, which could result in them landing that next great role.

The second use of the Leadership Matrix in succession planning efforts isn't as pleasant, but it's necessary. Look at your Slackers, Square Pegs, Joyriders, and Stowaways. Those individuals aren't performing. If their poor results continue, you could end up with an open slot on your team. The Leadership Matrix can highlight roles that may soon be vacant, so you can identify successors for those possible vacancies. You have a responsibility to your team and your organization to keep things running smoothly and prevent business interruptions. If someone on your team departs—either by his choice or yours—his work still needs to get done. In the short term, it will get distributed across your team, which increases the burden they carry. That's not a sustainable approach. Get a replacement into that role quickly. The longer it takes you to do so, the more stress you put on your team and the more operational risk you create for the organization because of an increased likelihood that something will go wrong. If you use the Leadership Matrix to plan for possible vacancies, you can fill those positions and get back to full strength sooner.

Career Pathing

Most people want to know where their career is headed. In dozens of polls we've conducted and in hundreds of conversations we've had, there's a resounding theme of people wanting growth opportunities. The clearer you can make their possible future paths, the easier it is for them to decide to stay with your organization—or leave, as the case may be. The Leadership Matrix is a useful tool for identifying how team members should be moving around to different roles in your organization. You can use the insights you generate from your assessment to let your team members know what their trajectory looks like in both the short and long term. For example, Rising Stars should be moving on and up. Square Pegs should be considering other roles that better fit their skills. Domain Masters should know what staying put in their role looks like and the impact that has on their compensation. The more clearly you can explain to your team members where they are, where you think they should be—and where they want to be—as well as the behaviors they need to change to get there, the higher the likelihood they succeed in doing so.

Incorporate these career-path discussions into your regular performance-review process. Give your team members a perspective on where they've been that year and where that places them on the Leadership Matrix. Next, spell out where you think they can be. Not everyone will be an Exemplar, so be sure to manage expectations appropriately. Give them a sense for the behaviors you expect to see them demonstrate to get to that new performance level. Discuss possible roles and projects that will build their skills and show they're capable of delivering the expected results. Evaluate the capabilities they need to have for that next step in their career progression.

Agree upon how the two of you will work together to build those skills throughout the coming year. You and your team members need to be thoughtful and plan their career paths well. Focus your efforts on building skills to prepare them for their next career step. With a solid plan and focused execution, they'll be advancing to that next role at a pace you're both happy with.

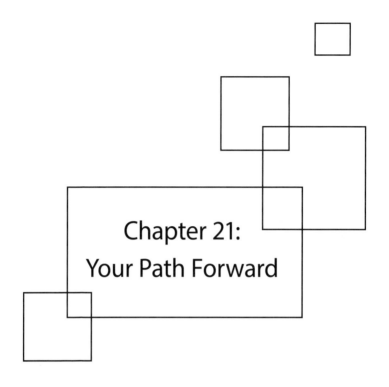

Chapter 21:
Your Path Forward

Your leadership success hinges upon your ability to get your people to perform well. There aren't enough hours in the day for you to equally dedicate your focus to every individual on your team. The only *real* choice you have is to be intentional about where you spend that time and energy—and where you don't. The Leadership Matrix is your key to creating your own leadership-capital allocation formula. It can help you make difficult decisions about where to focus and where not to. Once you've made that determination, use the approaches we've offered for how to lead your team members to more "efficient" boxes on the matrix. Getting more output for less input enables you to be more efficient and have a better chance of achieving a reasonable work-life balance.

Shifting where you invest your time and energy will take some getting used to. Spend time with those who need it. Build self-sufficiency for those who don't. Engage your team members and give them the type of leadership they need as *individuals*. The Leadership Matrix and its associated leadership approaches will point you in the right direction toward achieving great results. In the process, your team members will be challenged to perform at a higher level. Whether they're Slackers or Rising Stars, you'll be able to lead them toward a more fulfilling role.

The beauty of the Leadership Matrix is its simplicity, and that you can use it in a host of situations. From taking on a new team to rebuilding a dysfunctional one, you'll be well equipped to tackle the challenge. We encourage you to try it in any people-leadership situation you face. To get comfortable with using it, reflect on teams you've led in the past. Answer the assessment questions about those team members and see if they land where you think they should on the matrix. We're betting you won't be surprised at the results. Your former team members will most likely fit into one of the eight behavioral types we've included in this book. When you see the Leadership Matrix matches your own personal experience, you should feel more confident using it in new situations.

The more you use the Leadership Matrix, the more intuitive it will become for you. We find ourselves using it in casual coaching conversations without even realizing we're doing it. As people describe their team members, we're able to categorize the behavior and give guidance for how to lead them. People ask us, "How did you come up with that recommendation so fast? It's like you know this person as well as I do!" The answer, of course, is we're able to recognize behavioral patterns and apply what we know from the Leadership Matrix to that particular situation. If you practice applying this enough, you'll be able to do this too.

Remember—all you have to do is answer a few straightforward questions and assess the behaviors of the people you're leading. Once you do, you can build a plan and begin driving performance improvement immediately. If you're successful in these efforts, you'll see your team's behaviors change in a positive way. Those changes will show up as better results, more motivated team members, and better interpersonal relationships. Who doesn't want to lead a team like that? So forget the clichéd notion of "thinking outside the box." The *real* answer to guiding your team to exceptional performance requires you to lead *inside* the box.

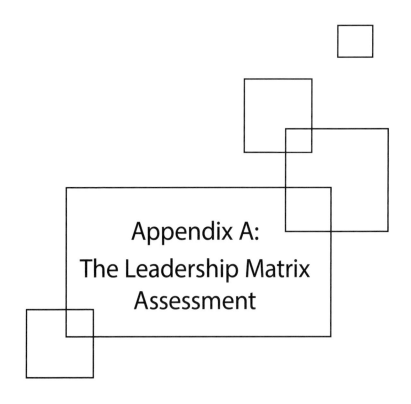

Appendix A:
The Leadership Matrix
Assessment

To assess your team members' behaviors, examine how much leadership capital you're investing in them. Ask yourself the questions in this Appendix about their delivery of results. Evaluate their behavior throughout the past year to avoid a "recency effect" skewing the results. As you answer the questions, write down instances of observed behaviors to support your answer. Having concrete examples allows you to identify targeted behaviors to change, or maintain, as the case might be. Those observations guide your provision of feedback and coaching to that team member so he knows what behaviors he needs to change. For each dimension or question, we've offered an example of clear documentation of an observed behavior. There are examples of both good and bad behaviors to give you a sense for how you can document your team members' performance.

For convenience's sake, we've made this assessment available online at *www.leadinsidethebox.com/assessment.* In the online version, you can answer all the following questions, include comments to support your answers, and get a custom report on that team member emailed directly to you. You can assess as many team members as you like and use the reports as documentation of their progress.

Input (Leadership Capital)— The 12 "Leadership Services"

Answer **yes** if this team member uses the service in question more than expected.

1. **Directing**—Planning, Prioritizing, and Coordinating
2. **Doing**—Deciding, Motivating, and Clearing
3. **Delivering**—Monitoring, Correcting, and Repairing
4. **Developing**—Training, Coaching, and Promoting

Directing

Planning: Leaders translate their vision for the organization into team goals and further into individual goals. Your team members should be responsible for determining *how* to achieve their goals. Are you spending more energy than you should managing this person's individual goal definition and how she'll achieve those goals?

Example: Tim missed his budget this quarter and came to me with a recovery plan that only recaptured half of the shortfall. After sharing his results, he said, "I don't know what to do to fix this." When I asked about his plan to close the gap, he said, "Can't you provide me with relief from your other teams?"

Example: Alan helps his colleagues to identify risks to their budgets. He works with them to put contingency plans in place in the event of negative results. He budgets conservatively and identifies all the initiatives and tactics for achieving his goals with room to spare.

Prioritizing: Determining priorities is important. A large consumer of leadership capital is changing priorities and then reallocating resources accordingly. Team member behaviors can force leaders to reprioritize work and shift resources. Does this person need you to cover his shortfalls—by reprioritizing work and shifting resources—more than he should?

Example: Rebecca often miscalculates the resources she needs. The most recent example is that she requested an additional $57,500 beyond her budget of $423,000 for two additional contractors to complete her project.

Example: Gail has never asked for additional resources to complete any of her work in the last two and a half years. She plans her work meticulously and finds creative ways to follow her constraints when things don't go according to plan.

Coordinating: Leaders provide their team members with broader organizational perspectives and make connections for them. Your people should be able to make many of these connections themselves. Does this person require you to spend more time and energy than you should helping her coordinate with others across the organization?

Example: Keith often complains that he feels "left out of the loop" and that he never has support for his projects. I frequently have to remind him to assess his stakeholders and seek their input. On five occasions in the past six months I had to insist he set meetings with other departmental leaders to get their perspectives on his primary project.

Example: Mark invests time in building relationships within the team by scheduling "lunch and learn" sessions with his colleagues every other week. His goal in doing so is learning about what his peers are working on. Mark manages a "Key Stakeholder Relationship Matrix" for how he interacts and influences people across the company. He's done so for more than a year.

Doing

Deciding: Leaders make decisions that can't or shouldn't be made by their team members. Your team members should differentiate between decisions they escalate to you and ones they shouldn't. Are you helping this person make many decisions he should be making on his own?

Example: Don made four purchasing decisions this year that were well above his level of decision-making authority. He was aware of his decision limits and still elected to make the decision without getting my approval. One such decision delayed a major project by three weeks because of problems he caused for our vendor partner. These were decisions he should not have made.

Example: Fiona always adheres to team decision-making criteria. When a decision needs to be escalated, she ensures it gets to the right decision-maker within 24 hours. When she has the authority to make a decision, she does so quickly and keeps me informed of her choices.

Motivating: Leaders motivate people to do things they don't want to do. However, leaders should expect a certain level of self-motivation from their team members. Do you have to drive this person to do her work more than you should?

Example: Brooke doesn't take the initiative to start working on tasks despite being given clear assignments and deadlines. Every Monday morning I sit down with her and either offer a reward if she completes her deliverables for the week (e.g., positive report in her review) or outline consequences (e.g., having to stay late) if she doesn't complete them.

Example: Jillian is a true self-starter. She starts her work on her own initiative and drives projects to completion with little supervision required. I have never had to use a disciplinary tool to motivate her to get her work done.

Clearing: People run into roadblocks to getting their job done. They should be able to overcome some of these obstacles by themselves. Do you find yourself spending more of your time, energy, or goodwill than you should clearing obstacles for this person?

Example: Jim was dismissive of the steering committee's concerns when he said, "I don't think you folks understand how this works. It'll be fine." That one comment required me to spend 30 to 60 minutes with each steering committee member discussing their concerns. He should have acknowledged their issue and worked to overcome the objection himself.

Example: Laurie routinely involves key stakeholders in decision meetings, incorporates their input, and resolves conflicts quickly. She demonstrated this on Project COYOTE last month. I have not had to intervene on any of her projects this year.

Delivering

Monitoring: Leaders track team progress against goals by checking in with team members to ensure their work is getting done. If you have to check in more frequently with one team member than others, he's requiring more monitoring from you. Do you have to manage this team member's tasks more than you should to ensure his work is getting done?

Example: Dave often begins work on new tasks that haven't been approved, and does so at the expense of his core responsibilities. This month I had to make him stop work on six new initiatives he launched on his own. I then needed to insist he focus on his primary deliverable of making his required sales calls.

Example: Kim effectively prioritizes her work on her Project Tracking Dashboard. She updates the tracker weekly or as projects statuses change and apprises me of status changes at least once a week.

Correcting: Team members are responsible for checking their work for completeness and correctness. If you're finding more mistakes in someone's work than you should, she's overly reliant on you for quality checking. Are you spending more time than you should checking, correcting, or completing her work?

Example: Andrew turns in incomplete or error-ridden work at the last minute, then complains he doesn't have time to fix it. The last time this happened he said, "Can you just make the corrections you want? That'll be faster than you telling me the changes and me making them. That seems like the best approach since this is due tomorrow." I had to spend all night redoing the majority of his report or it would have been late.

Example: Heather's work is always mistake-free. In the past year I have corrected fewer than 10 typos total in the hundreds of documents she has worked on and I have never found a calculation error.

Repairing: Team members may deliver acceptable results but their approach to getting those results creates problems, such as damaging relationships with others. You have to repair damaged relationships caused by your team member's behavior. Are you spending more time than you should repairing problems caused by this team member?

Example: Peter talks about people behind their backs and causes conflict. I've had no fewer than six conversations this month with his team members and peers to undo the damage his words have done.

Example: Behram builds relationships with key stakeholders across the organization and acts as an ambassador for our team. He serves on four cross-functional steering committees where he represents our team's perspective. He's built relationships with leaders in IT, Finance, and HR.

Developing

Training: Leaders must teach team members new skills and ensure they receive the training they need. When you teach and train your team members, it's not a one-off event. You'll need to retrain them until they're competent in the task. Are you teaching this person material he should already know and training him on skills he should already have?

Example: Barb submitted large deliverables five times in the last two months and all of them required considerable editing and correcting. She needed me to explain basic financial principles to her on seven occasions despite the fact that she's a "certified expert" in the field.

Example: Lynn delivers error-free work with little to no supervision required. When she doesn't know how to do something, she researches how to do it and then makes it happen.

Coaching: Team members need their leader's guidance in difficult situations. Leaders provide coaching to get team members through their challenges, build their confidence, and help them overcome obstacles—both professional and personal. Does this person constantly come to you asking for coaching on issues she should be able to resolve on her own?

Example: Ricky abuses my open-door policy. He stops by my office unannounced at least four times a week saying he needs coaching on an issue. When he explains the problem, it's clear he's put little thought into generating possible solutions on his own. Many of the issues he raises are of little significance, such as asking for suggestions on the best colors to use for coding his Outlook calendar appointments.

Example: Lesli is judicious in making coaching requests, and when she does, she arrives fully prepared to discuss her challenge. She types up an issue sheet that includes the problem, solutions she's considered, and key questions she has for me. She's done this for every coaching request she's made of me this year.

Promoting: Leaders advance their team members' careers, position them well in the organization, and build the organization's talent pool. Although leaders can formulate a plan for career advancement, it's up to the team member to drive the creation of that plan and execute it. Does this person want career advancement but not take ownership of his development so he relies upon you instead?

Example: Karen complains that she hasn't been promoted, but she's failed to generate her career-path plan. Her self-appraisal was poorly written and her Development Action Plan only had three ideas listed on it with no details. Simply writing "training," "get coaching," and "participate in industry networking groups" is not a development plan. I had to spend three hours with her this week reworking her plan.

Example: Sri has done an exemplary job on his development planning. He's identified three possible future roles, defined the skills required for each, and conducted a self-assessment on his readiness for the role. He's laid out an actionable development plan for how he could acquire those skills throughout the next six to 12 months.

Output (Team Member Results)

Use the following questions to assess your team members' output. Record your results on tables such as the ones we provide at the end of this Appendix.

Quantity: What is the quantity of results compared to what is expected or asked of them? (High/Medium/Low)

Example: Low—Tim missed his revenue target by $18,000 in January and his recovery plan for February only makes up $8,700 of that shortfall.

Example: High—Alan came in 11% ahead of the revenue plan for last quarter and is on track to exceed his goals by 7% next quarter.

Quality: How is the quality of their final work versus what is expected? (High/Medium/Low)

Example: Low—Andrew's work is always full of math and accounting errors. The last four financial analyses he submitted were inaccurate and needed substantial corrections. The conclusions he draws from his analyses are often incorrect at worst and only marginally insightful at best. Compared to his peers, the quality of his work lags significantly.

Example: High—Paul consistently exceeds high quality expectations. He recently created a set of training materials for a new course. Not only did he create interesting and clear materials, but he also created a companion facilitator guide to improve other facilitators' delivery of the program. This additional guide was his own idea, and his colleagues now deliver better programs because of it.

Timeliness: How timely is the work they deliver versus expected deadlines or durations? (High/Medium/Low)

Example: Low—Rebecca has trouble meeting deadlines because she doesn't plan well. Her plans always reflect a best-case scenario; if everything goes perfectly. Often projects go much worse than she planned for. Her current project is a perfect example—it's already overdue by six weeks and it's only a three-month project.

Example: High—William delivered his last few projects up to three weeks early. He communicated the accelerated completion dates to everyone involved so they could better plan their own projects and shift their priorities given the additional time they would now have. He did all of this in spite of being shorthanded by one person for two of these projects.

Intangibles (a): To what degree do they improve morale in their immediate team? (High/Medium/Low)

Example: Low—Jo always finds the negative aspect of a situation and makes sure everyone on the team knows how bad things are. During her portion of my team meetings, her updates always start with "Top 5 Risks and Issues," even though her area of responsibility is managing the new innovation pipeline. In almost any interaction where she's asked for her thoughts on a new idea, she begins her reply with "No, because..." Her coworkers have begun avoiding her and referring to her as "No-go Jo" because of these behaviors.

Example: High—Gina sees the positive in everything and leads others to do the same. She instituted a weekly "achievement celebration" email announcement in which she promotes people's accomplishments from the prior week. She manages a blog for the department where she highlights good news, new ideas, and personal accomplishments. She updates that information several times a week. She volunteered to take on these activities in addition to her operational responsibilities. Everyone in the department looks forward to her updates.

Intangibles (b): To what extent do they improve relationships with stakeholders and colleagues outside their immediate team? (High/Medium/Low)

Example: Low—Keith does not build relationships within the team, let alone in the broader organization. He rarely interacts with his colleagues unless it's required of him. When he does, it's strictly a transactional interaction. Keith spends the majority of his time in his office with the door closed and only interacts with his peers when they reach out to him to seek his approval on a project.

Example: High—Anirban is a "connector"—he knows everyone in the division as well as what they're working on. On almost a weekly basis he makes introductions and suggestions to people about who they should reach out to because he sees an opportunity for those individuals to collaborate. He is widely known as the first person to go to if you have a question about "who knows something about this topic?" because the majority of the time he can make exactly the right connection.

Input: Leadership Capital (YES/NO)	Team Member #1	Team Member #2	Team Member #3	Team Member #4
Planning				
Prioritizing				
Coordinating				
Deciding				
Motivating				
Clearing				
Monitoring				
Correcting				
Repairing				
Training				
Coaching				
Promoting				
TOTAL				
CATEGORY (High or Low)				

Do they require too much of this service from you?

Yes = 1, No = 0

Output: Team Member Results (H/M/L)	Team Member #1	Team Member #2	Team Member #3	Team Member #4
Quantity of Results				
Quality of Results				
Timeliness				
Morale-Building				
Relationship-Building				
TOTAL				
CATEGORY (High or Low)				

High = 2, Medium = 1, Low = 0

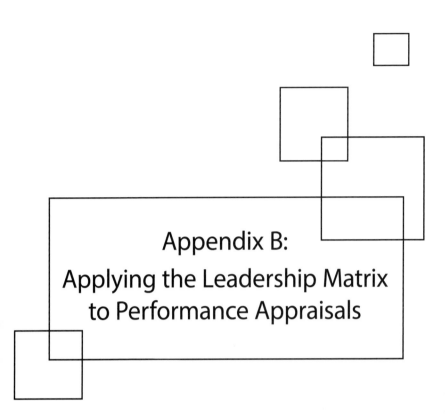

Appendix B:
Applying the Leadership Matrix
to Performance Appraisals

Some common performance appraisal pitfalls are associated with each behavioral type in the Leadership Matrix, so we'd like to offer thoughts on what to watch out for as you write performance appraisals for team members in each box. Once you've plotted each team member on the Leadership Matrix, it's useful to compare their position in the boxes versus previous performance assessments they've received. This will help you vet the previous assessments in a new way. You can communicate the results of your Leadership Matrix assessment to them in a context they'll understand. You'll also see if you've fallen into some dangerous performance appraisal traps. Those traps include the following:

❑ **Domain Masters** can be underrated because leaders don't feel an urgency to rate them at the highest levels. Domain Masters aren't pushing for the next promotion, so getting the highest rating is not at the top of *their* mind. Because they don't require much time and energy from their leaders, ensuring they're happy may not be at the top of *their leader's* mind. Domain Masters derive intrinsic value from being great at a job they enjoy. They may not need or ask for much more than the ability to excel in their role as a reward. Be sure you're rating Domain Masters fairly and compensating them accordingly. Look at their results side by side with others on the team and rate them where they deserve to be rated.

❑ **Rising Stars** can be underrated if tenure in a position is weighted too heavily in your organization's performance-appraisal culture. If you hear something like the following in performance discussions, your culture creates this underrating risk: "She's only been in the role for a year. We always make people wait two years before they're eligible for promotion." If a Rising Star sees a significant amount of "dead" time that he'll have to suffer through before he can get promoted, he might be tempted to join another organization that doesn't have arbitrary promotion waiting periods. If a less-deserving colleague—such as a Steamroller or Squeaky Wheel—is promoted ahead of him, your Rising Star might head for the door. Avoid this risk by taking tenure out of the discussion and evaluate your Rising Stars' readiness based solely upon results and competencies.

❑ **Squeaky Wheels** can be overrated because they're so needy. If leaders rate a Squeaky Wheel below the highest rating, they know they're going to hear a stream of complaints from their Squeaky Wheel. To avoid trouble, a leader might be tempted to take the path of least resistance and give a Squeaky Wheel a higher rating than she deserves. That rating could even be on par with an Exemplar's rating. After all, the Squeaky Wheel is producing output at a high level, albeit with an inordinate amount of help from their leader. By rating her higher than he should, a leader risks rewarding the Squeaky Wheel's badgering behaviors. Leaders also risk alienating their Exemplar colleagues who also produce high output. Compare the Squeaky Wheel's results to the Exemplar's to ensure you're not rating this team member higher than you should.

❑ **Steamrollers** can be overrated because their interactions can be intimidating. Leaders may want to avoid the confrontation that would result if they didn't give a Steamroller a high rating. By rating them higher than they deserve, a leader risks rewarding Steamrollers' negative behaviors. A Steamroller will see a high rating as an official stamp of approval that his behavior is acceptable—or even desirable! That may embolden him to be even more aggressive. Even worse, promoting a Steamroller sends a strong message to others in the organization that teamwork is not valued. Give Steamrollers the accolades for great results but penalize them for their bad behaviors. If you never call it out, they'll never change it.

❏ **Joyriders** can be overrated because their leaders overvalue the enthusiasm they bring to work every day. Leaders may also overrate them to avoid the difficult conversation that could result if they rate a Joyrider lower than expected. Because Joyriders have crafted their own goals around activities they most enjoy doing, they believe they're delivering great results. If their leader discounts the value of the projects they're working on, Joyriders might argue for a higher rating given their perceptions of how important their work is. Weak leaders cave in to this pressure and award higher ratings than Joyriders deserve. Avoid these issues by tracking back to their goals that were agreed upon at the beginning of the year and assess them against that standard instead of evaluating the work they've done in lieu of pursuing their objectives.

❑ **Stowaways** can be overrated because they've become masters at earning passing grades with minimum effort. They take maximum advantage of the general desire many leaders have to avoid conflict. They keep their heads down and make sure they don't provoke any negative attention that could convince their leaders to rate their "below expectations" results appropriately. Make their appraisal as objective as possible. Compare their results to fact-based metrics and assign ratings commensurate with their performance relative to those goals. It's hard to dispute the numbers.

❑ **Slackers** can be overrated because, even though they don't deliver results, they're effective at influencing others to perceive them the way they perceive themselves. Their true performance failures are masked by the veneer of being smart or hard-working. Leaders may avoid the debate they know will ensue if they rate a Slacker poorly. Steer clear of this hazard by comparing a Slacker's results to an Exemplar's. In the Slacker's mind, she sees herself as an Exemplar. Burst that bubble by showing her what a real Exemplar's results look like.

❑ **Square Pegs** can be overrated because leaders blame themselves for the Square Peg's lack of skills. If a leader sees it as his fault that he placed the Square Peg in a role she's not suited for, he'll have a hard time assigning a low rating to her. Realize that you have a responsibility to let Square Pegs know where their performance rates and that you'll help them improve by building their skills with them. Failure to deliver an honest rating could make them complacent and give them a false sense of security about their capabilities. Deliver the tough message and follow it with the plan for how you're going to invest in their development.

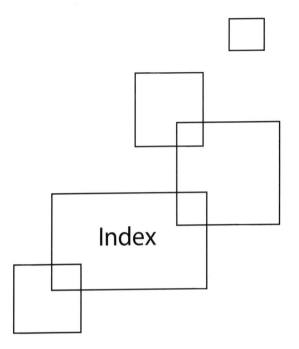

Index

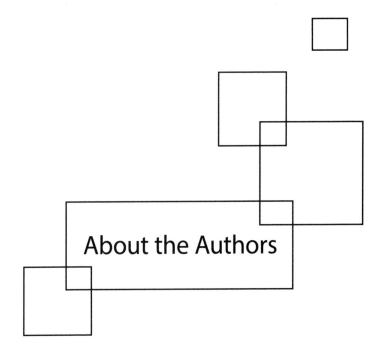

About the Authors

Victor Prince

Victor Prince has more than 20 years of experience in corporate and government leadership positions. He earned an MBA from the Wharton School of the University of Pennsylvania and a BA (magna cum laude) from American University in Washington DC. After Wharton, Victor was a consultant with Bain & Company, where he developed business strategy for clients in the United States, Great Britain, France, and Spain. Most recently, Victor was the Chief Operating Officer of the Consumer Financial Protection Bureau (CFPB), where he managed a division of more than 300 staff and $100 million of budget for the new federal regulatory agency. Prior to the CFPB, Victor was a member of Washington DC Mayor Fenty's cabinet as the Director of CapStat, the performance accountability program for the $10 billion local government. Before his time in public service, Victor worked in the private sector as a marketing executive with Capital One and Webs.com. Victor is Managing Director of DiscoveredLOGIC (*www.discoveredlogic.com*), a strategy consulting and training firm, where he serves clients in the United States and internationally.

Mike Figliuolo

Mike Figliuolo is an honor graduate of the United States Military Academy at West Point, where he graduated in the top 5 percent of his class. He served in the U.S. Army as an armor officer. After several years of leading soldiers in the army, Mike spent time in corporate America as a consultant at McKinsey & Company and as an executive in various roles at Capital One Financial and the Scotts Miracle-Gro Company.

Mike is the founder and managing director of *thought*LEADERS, LLC (*www.thoughtleadersllc.com*). He and his team train leaders at world-class companies on topics of leadership, strategy, communications, innovation, and other critical business skills. He's also the author of *One Piece of Paper: The Simple Approach to Powerful, Personal Leadership*—a book that shows leaders how to be authentic by sharing their personal story on a single page. A highly sought-after speaker and trainer, Mike has delivered his message to thousands of leaders around the world through keynote presentations, classroom instruction, and personal coaching.

Mike's clients include Abbott, Discover, OhioHealth, Visa, Heinz, Abbvie, Cardinal Health, Huntington, Bristol-Myers Squibb, Nationwide, ServiceMASTER, and many other industry-leading firms.